The Poetics of Political Thinking

Duke University Press   Durham and London   2006

DAVIDE PANAGIA

The

Poetics

of Political

Thinking

© 2006 Duke University Press
All rights reserved

Designed by C. H. Westmoreland
Typeset in Janson
by Tseng Information Systems, Inc.
Library of Congress Cataloging-
in-Publication Data
appear on the last printed page
of this book.

For my father,

VINCENZO PANAGIA

(1939–2000)

In memoriam

Contents

GRAZIE ix

INTRODUCTION: Images of Political Thought 1

1 Delicate Discriminations: Thomas Hobbes's Science of Politics 19

2 The Banality of the Negative: Gilles Deleuze's Ethics of the Problem 45

3 The Beautiful and the Sublime in Rawls and Rancière 68

4 The Force of Political Argument: Habermas, Hazlitt, and the Essay 96

AFTERWORD: *Les Sans Papiers*, or No Vox Populi, Vox Dei 119

NOTES 125

BIBLIOGRAPHY 151

INDEX 161

Grazie

This book is in every way a collaborative effort, and chief among my collaborators is William Connolly. His willingness to engage my ideas, along with his insights and encouragements, is second only to his friendship. Frances Ferguson was kind enough to let me participate in one of her seminars at a crucial moment, when I was beginning to formulate the ideas outlined in these pages. The collaboration from that one class, that then became many classes and even more conversations, has made all the difference. Dick Flathman never let me say or write a word without having a characteristically pugnacious response ready. Kirstie McClure not only taught me the value of a historically inflected mode of political thinking, she also taught me how to teach. Her exemplarity remains constant.

While I was a master's student at Oxford, Michael Freeden's guidance helped me understand the value of grace against adversity. Ken Reshaur, my undergraduate mentor at the University of Manitoba, introduced me to the study of political theory and all its eccentricities—so blame him.

At Johns Hopkins, where this project began, opportunities for dissensus were plenty. Participation in the Center for Research on Culture and Literature, the Graduate Forum, and the Political and Moral Thought Program offered many occasions for critical engagement.

Amanda Anderson, Jane Bennett, Milton Cummings, Michael Fried, John Marshall, Walter Benn Michaels, Anthony Pagden, and Gabrielle Spiegel offered comments, criticisms, and suggestions and have encouraged my research interests throughout.

Outside of Hopkins, I have had the good fortune of befriending many others who have acted, in their own ways, as advisors. Jacques Rancière had the misfortune of having me for an enthusiast. With characteristic kindness, he has responded to all my invitations and exchanges in friendship. I first encountered Seyla Benhabib's generosity in her seminar at the 1999 meeting of the School of Criticism and Theory at Cornell University, which was, dare I say, critical. Generous also is the continued support and counsel of Bill Chaloupka, Tom Dumm, Joshua Foa Dienstag, Bonnie Honig, Sharon Krause, Pratap Bhanu Mehta, Paul Patton, Michael Sandel, Mort Schoolman, Tracy Strong, Stephen White, Melissa Williams, and Linda Zerilli. I am indebted to them all for lending a thoughtful eye and ear.

My indebtedness also extends to my classmates and friends: Arash Abizadeh, Jacqueline Best, Scott Black, Maggie Brown, Theo Davis, Michaele Ferguson, Jason Frank, Jennet Kirkpatrick, Jeff Lomonaco, Larissa MacFarquhar, Patchen Markell, Stefanie Markovits, Edit Penchina, John D. Rockefeller V, Paul Saurette, Kam Shapiro, Lisa Siraganian, Verity Smith, Dan Stone, Miriam Ticktin, Kathy Trevenan, Paul Vogt, and Paul Winke. I extend a special note of gratitude to Peter Beinart, Erez Kalir, and Siddhartha Mukherjee for their continued loyalty and friendship, as well as to Barton Beebe, Patricia De Luca, Morris Karamazyn, Salim Loxley, Glen Mitchell, Riccardo Pelizzo, Matt and Tyler Pierce, Elisabetta Povoledo, Amrit Singh, Lucas Swaine, and Ananya Vajpeyi for the same.

Courtney Berger of Duke University Press witnessed the beginnings of this project, way back when. Since then, her support as both friend and editor has been singular.

While revising the manuscript, I had the pleasure of spending a charmed year as Social Sciences and Humanities Research Council of Canada Post-doctoral Fellow at the Center for Reformation and Renaissance Studies at the University of Toronto, Victoria College. I am especially grateful to William Bowen, Konrad Eisenbichler, Olga

Pugliese, Guido Pugliese, Manuela Scarci, and Kim Yates for their attention and support.

At Trent University I have been welcomed by colleagues both in the cultural studies department and throughout this vibrant institution. Most notably, I wish to extend my appreciation to Doug Torgerson, the director of Trent's Center for the Study of Theory, Culture, and Politics, who not only championed my nomination as Canada Research Chair in Cultural Studies, but also deferred his sabbatical year so as to ensure my smooth transition back onto Canadian soil. Further thanks extend to zsuzsa baross, Jonathan Bordo, Constantin Boundas, Richard Dellamora, Charmaine Eddy, John Fekete, Victoria Hollinger, Elaine Stavro, Andrew Wernick, and Nancy Legate for their hospitality. Another Trentonian worthy of note is Katharine Wolfe, who took on the arduous task of helping me revise, edit, and index the book.

I thank the publishers and editors of *Polity* and *Political Theory* for allowing me to publish some of the material that originally appeared in their journals (chapters 1 and 4, respectively). Chapter 1 was presented at the Western Political Science Association meeting (2001), whereas chapters 3 and 4 were presented at the American Political Science Association (2002 and 2000, respectively). I am especially grateful to the reviewers at Duke University Press for their excellent comments and criticisms on earlier versions of the manuscript.

Gratitudes expressed in the acknowledgments of one's first book resemble an acceptance speech: there is limited time before the music starts playing, inevitably resulting in omissions. To those whose generosity remains unnoted, know that it is not unacknowledged.

One group, however, cannot go without mention—my family, for whom my gratitude is unceasing: my mother, Maria Luisa, my father, Vincenzo, and my brother, Marcello. We immigrated to Winnipeg, Canada, in 1977 from Brescia, Italy. The pages that follow are witness to that initial encounter with dissensus that, in no small way, we continue to share and negotiate to this day.

Who that is busy to measure and compass
The heaven and earth and all the world large
Describing the climates and folk of every place
He is a fool. —SEBASTIAN BRANT

There is a place where Contrarieties are
equally True. —WILLIAM BLAKE

Never have two men judged alike of the same thing, and it is impossible to find two opinions exactly similar, not only in different men, but in the same man at different times.
—MICHEL DE MONTAIGNE

Taste as a principle of "organization"—that is, taste decides not only the question of which things we like or how the world is to look and sound, but also *who* in the world belongs together. —HANNAH ARENDT

Introduction

IMAGES OF POLITICAL THOUGHT

> Unfortunately nothing is so difficult to represent by literary means as a man thinking. —ROBERT MUSIL

Aesthetics and Politics

Contemporary political theory is nothing if not puzzling with respect to what is political and what counts as thinking politically. Hannah Arendt, noting a "curiously difficult problem of the relationship between politics and philosophy,"[1] once remarked that politics, by its very nature, is often at odds with truth, and that the best politics can do is provide sound judgments in the form of opinions, not truths. Today we encounter an equally curious corollary to Arendt's observation: the principal virtue of an elected official in a modern democratic polity is to not be political. This moral obligation evaluates the term *political* negatively and associates it with such well-worn governmental practices as partisanship, pork-barreling, pandering to group interests, and so on. Not unlike the term *ideology* during the 1970s and 1980s, an accusation by one's adversaries or by the popular media of "thinking politically" is tantamount to a personal insult, immediately challenging one's moral rectitude.

Attempting to rethink the value of politics, contemporary political theorists have articulated contesting accounts of the political over the past several decades. A series of encounters between thinkers from a variety of academic disciplines and theoretical orientations ensued. Indeed, if we are to continue to imagine that political life, like a linguistic system, involves the formation of relations among entities, then it is of little surprise to find literary theorists, anthropologists, historians, cultural theorists, and others as intellectual contributors to ongoing debates about the nature of political arrangements. As it turns out, then, political theory's confusion regarding the semantic content of its two defining terms was not (and is not) a limitation for political reflection at all; it, rather, infuses and expresses the nature of politics itself.

In these pages I examine the images of political thought that helped spark one of the most lively debates in political theory in recent years, the liberal/poststructural debate. Proponents of this debate typically focus on the function and legitimacy of moral norms for political action. From the liberal camp, we learn that moral norms are required to justify actions and beliefs; on the poststructural side, norms are viewed as *normalizing* and therefore subject to suspicion. In both cases, however, assumptions about the openness or closure of language set the stage for the image of thought advanced.

I wish to challenge the predominance of this moral image of thought in contemporary political theory by introducing the possibility that our understandings of political life are informed by our aesthetic sensibilities. Thus, I refer to a thinker's ideas as an *image* of political thought, rather than simply an argument or theory, so as to bring out the multiple layers of signification composing ideas. Ideas are more multivalent than epistemic accounts of them suggest. The images they present, the impressions they emit, and the connections they ascertain all point to strata of value that extend well beyond their value as a philosophical argument. "The sign or point of departure for that which forces thought," Gilles Deleuze once noted, "is the coexistence of contraries."[2] In what follows I reconsider the complexity of ideas—

a complexity of contraries that parallels the coexistence of dissimilars that characterize democratic political life.

My use of the term *image* to refer to the form and content of ideas might be construed as polemical. The word *image* immediately situates us in the midst of one of the most enduring concerns in the history of political thought that helps explain what Arendt meant by the "curiously difficult problem of the relationship between politics and philosophy." An image is not a truth but a semblance of it, as its etymology from the Latin *imitari* suggests; an image is a copy that pretends to be something other than what it is.[3] To refer to a political idea in terms of the semblance of truth might suggest to some that there are no truths in politics, merely falsities. Though this may be a valid first impression—one that is immediately available, given contemporary apprehensions about theoretical and moral relativism—I invite the reader to look beyond the polemical incitement of my semantic choices and consider the extent to which image, knowledge, and political power are intimately related with one another.

Plato's allegory of the cave in book 7 of *The Republic* is as good a place as any to begin such considerations. The shackled individuals sitting facing the wall, we recall, view images projected by the faint light of a flickering fire behind them. They are, in fact, bound creatures who require liberation from their bondage. The first thing we learn from this founding image in the history of political thought is that knowledge and freedom are intimately related and the ability to know things—to determine their epistemological veracity—is linked with justice. As we read Socrates's words further and pay particular attention to Plato's stylistics, we notice a paradox at play: the tale presents an image of political thought that is at once cognitively challenging and somatically disturbing. For the Greeks, to be shackled meant to be a slave, and to be a slave meant exclusion from the life of the polis. Plato's account of the illumination that comes from knowledge relies on an image of imprisonment that conjures up the kinds of negative sensations associated with political exclusion and exile.[4]

Yet liberation from such oppressive tutelage is not as placid as the illumination metaphor allows. The light of truth is not the kind of light we seek for vacation purposes, a soothing light that distracts us from the stresses of daily living. Plato's Socrates is much more violent when referring to the passage from image to truth: "Let him be dragged away by force up the rough and steep incline of the cave's passageway, held fast until he is hauled out into the light of the sun," Socrates commands. Then he asks: "Would not such a rough passage be painful? Would he not resent the experience?"[5] Indeed he might. Enlightenment requires the kind of force that drags the individual by the hair, like a child unwilling to go to school on the first warm day of spring. Eventually, Socrates explains, this person would get used to the light; illumination becomes an addictive habit that compels our stranger to "look at the sun as it is, in its own domain, and so be able to see what it is really like," Socrates concludes.

So there we have it. The passage from an image to the thing-in-itself is a passage from imprisonment to freedom, from the bondage of the image to the liberation of knowledge. Yet we must ask ourselves: What is this force that does the work of compelling? Who or what is doing the dragging? Moreover, what role does resentment play in this narrative of foundation? The answers to such questions are not easily available. From one perspective, the history of political reflection since Plato is an attempt to at least address if not resolve the burden of these questions. I am not concerned with this here. Rather, my interest is to note the role of sensation in Plato's account. Exposure to the light is a painful experience, not only physically but also emotionally and psychologically. It affects our senses as much as our mind, and it appeals to a level of discernment that enervates our somatic sensitivities as well as our cognitive faculties. In short, Plato's paradigm of illumination and justice, when considered from a stylistic as well as an expository point of view, betrays a commitment to a tacit aesthetic domain in matters of political reflection. The simultaneity of aesthetic and political reflection is a heritage that, despite a parallel history of its exorcism, contemporary accounts of the nature of political argument continue to shoulder.

This book examines the relationship between aesthetic and political forms of representation. My central claim is that aesthetic accounts of representation structure our understandings of how political representation works. The term *aesthetics* is relatively new; its usage, according to the *Oxford English Dictionary*, began late in the eighteenth century. The category of aesthetic inquiry, however, predates its linguistic coinage. Reflection on objects of beauty, art, and the sublime are—as Plato's writing evince—as old as reflections on the nature of justice, politics, and democratic life. By *aesthetics*, then, I refer to the tradition of reflection that turns to sense experience in order to pose the question of value: What is value and what are its modes of expression?

My analysis proceeds by means of what I call *a poetics of political thinking*. The literary term *poetics* comes to us, most famously, from Aristotle's *Poetics*, a philosophical treatise into the nature and principles of literature and, as Northrop Frye reminds us, "a theory of criticism whose principles apply to the whole of literature and account for every valid type of critical procedure."[6] I do not intend anything as comprehensive as Frye's definition of poetics recommends. Instead, I want to highlight two related objectives. The first is methodological: by "poetics of political thinking" I mean the coincidence of aesthetic and moral conceptions of value. When, in chapter 3, I suggest that John Rawls relies on poetics to justify his moral arguments, for instance, I mean that Rawls tacitly endorses an image of thought that inadvertently collapses the distinction between aesthetic and moral evaluation; that is, in his strategies of argumentation there is as much of an appeal to sense experience as to cognitive ratiocination. My second objective is prescriptive: by "poetics of political thinking" I also refer to the manner in which principles of aesthetic criticism may be successfully championed for political critique.[7]

Why, given the abundance of contemporary works on the relationship between aesthetics and politics, do I call to mind the reluctant stature of aesthetic judgment in contemporary political thought? One answer to this question is available in my reading of Plato's iconomachy: There is a fundamental distrust of aesthetics because the aesthetic realm is the realm of representation that, in Plato's hierarchies, is several strata away from the domain of truth. Indeed, Plato dislikes the poets almost as much as he dislikes the demos. Despite appreciations of aesthetic theories of value, there is a tendency to subsume aesthetic insights for the greater purpose of moral reflection.

The demands of intellectual clarity are such that, as Charles Larmore critically reminds us, "the function of art can no longer be to tell us something important about life or urge us to change the way we live, for these matters belong to the special provinces of knowledge and morality."[8]

There is another, more distressing, answer to my question: just as politics and truth are badly aligned, politics and aesthetics are equally disjointed. If the vicissitudes of political life may be rescued by normative ethics, it is often argued, then the indeterminacy of aesthetic judgment, with its apparent commitment to value as ornamental rather than practical, is pernicious for deliberative democracies, especially when political decision-making is at stake.[9] In short, there is a fear of the encroachment of the aesthetic into the normative that betrays a more profound fear of coercion: The temporality of suddenness that characterizes aesthetic experience creates a frightening state of stupor that interrupts cognitive reflection making people vulnerable to an other's will.[10] Given the lessons of Weimar Germany, then, we ought to fear the aestheticization of politics or, indeed, any performative account of politics.[11] Though I do not argue against the aestheticization of politics thesis directly, in the chapters that follow I show the difficulty in imagining what political life would be like without aesthetic accounts of value, and I suggest that aesthetic criticism, if nothing else, assists us in making an important political distinction between symbolic value and its deployment.

As I pursue it in the following pages, a poetics of political thinking addresses both the political and aesthetic complexities of representation. Though aesthetics is an expansive field of inquiry, my attention is limited to the literary use of language (hence my use of the term *poetics* rather than, say, *the figural* or *the musical*) precisely because of the prevailing emphasis in much contemporary political thought on the linguistic dimensions of deliberation in public life.[12] In so doing, I pursue an account of representation not exclusively bound to resemblance as an explanatory model. Representation, in other words, is understood as a process by which the intensity of difference in itself is acknowledged as an associational force in political life.

Mimetic accounts of representation rely on similitude as the associational force between two different objects. The clearest example of this is when we decipher the meaning of a metaphor and conclude that saying "every rose has its thorn,"[13] for instance, is like saying that love is as painful as it is beautiful. In doing so, we easily substitute one expression for another. The assumption here is that meaning exists independent of its mode of expression; or, better put, the fluidity of the substitutive operation suggests that the expression is secondary to the meaning itself. This sort of analysis focuses on what is similar between the two expressions and concludes that what makes the metaphor mean something—what links the two differing expressions—is their similitude despite the difference in expression, utterance, or images invoked. This account of metaphor and the associational basis of meaning constitutes what Paul Ricoeur calls a "substitution" theory of metaphor, where "every substitution of one term for another takes place within a sphere of resemblance."[14]

Borrowing from the works of Max Black, Monroe Beardsley, and Hans-Georg Gadamer, Ricoeur defends an interactive account of metaphor without dismissing the role of resemblance therein. Resemblance, Ricoeur argues, does indeed do part of the bridge work in metaphor. But the metaphorical operation—what he calls the power or metaphoricity of metaphor—implies a semantic innovation that a substitution theory, relying exclusively on resemblance and similitude, simply overlooks: "To say that metaphor is not drawn from anywhere," Ricoeur concludes, "is to recognize it for what it is: namely a momentary creation of language, a semantic innovation which does not have the status in the language as something already established, whether as a designation or as a connotation."[15] Designation and connotation are the properties of resemblance that assist in the understanding of metaphor. Yet they are insufficient in explaining the power of metaphor, because they do not address the innovatory qualities occurring in the metaphorical creation; qualities that Arendt, in her own distinct manner, refers to as the "human condition of natality" that in the case of action corresponds to the "fact of birth" and in the case of speech "corresponds to the fact of distinctness and is the actualization of the human condition of plurality."[16]

What distinguishes a substitution from an interaction account of metaphor is a commitment to difference as a force of distinction.[17] Whereas a substitution theory attends to resemblance as the predicative element in a metaphor, thereby endorsing identity as the associational principle sine qua non, an interactive account of metaphor looks to the clash of semantic fields that comprise the range of signification of a metaphorical utterance. In other words, an interactive theory focuses on the differentiating elements that constitute the metaphor; it looks to how the association of dissimilar entities occurs on the basis of their distinctive qualities rather than on what makes them similar. The power of association, then, rests on a differentiating intensity.

Keeping the distinction between substitution and interaction in mind, we conclude that a poetics of political thinking distinguishes between diversity as a quality or property of an object and difference as a force or intensity.[18] The human condition of plurality, the "fact of reasonable pluralism," is the fundamental dilemma of democratic politics. How is it the case, we ask ourselves, that we might have convergence in political matters given the diversity of opinions, cultures, and beliefs in a pluralist democracy? This restatement of the metaphysical problem of identity/difference (which, pace Rawls, is why politics cannot be simply "political and not metaphysical," as political thinking begins with the metaphysical question of the one and the many) addresses the difficulty of resolving the tension between unity and diversity. Whether we call it an "overlapping consensus," a "social contract," or a "lifeworld," each of these formulations is a restatement of the metaphysical conundrum of democratic politics that relies on a qualitative account of difference. In light of this, the most common tendency is to subsume diversity for the sake of unity, political stability, or agreement. This approach to the metaphysics of democracy eschews the possibility that difference is not a property assignable to individuals or groups but is, instead, the associational power that allows for politics to occur, a kind of energetic asymmetry that resides in things in an undesigned world. A poetics of political thinking attends to this metaphysical dimension of pluralism that looks to the interactive intensity of difference in itself as a source for novel forms of political association.

An Ethics of Aesthetics?

What can a poetics of political thinking offer current debates in democratic theory? For one thing, it helps us address the question of an ethics of aesthetics by highlighting the prominence of evaluation in democratic life. Perhaps the Theban herald in Euripides's *The Suppliants* stated the problem best: "How can the demos run the polis correctly when they do not assess the rhetor's speech correctly?"[19] The functioning of a well-organized political system and the assessment of public spectacles seem to go hand in hand; both require a discriminatory competence to help navigate the unquiet theatrocracy of democratic life.[20] Like Theseus, we too live in a culture of evaluation. Consider, in this regard, the prominence of the "top-ten" list as a currency of cultural capital: the AFI top-ten films of all time, *People* magazine's best and worst dressed lists, the top-ten songs on the Billboard charts, the top 10 percent of Texas high school students who have automatic acceptance to universities in the state. In our popular culture, the concept of value is assumed to be numerically verifiable and easily chartable along a vertical access that represents a public assessment of worth.[21]

By attending to the simultaneity of aesthetics and politics in such strategies of appraisal, we notice a substantive power dynamic at work in credentialing institutions like the top-ten list: The capacity and authority to dictate the standards of evaluation corresponds to a control over the processes of legitimation. If legitimacy of one's claims is a condition of political success, then the standards by which legitimacy is conferred stand in as the doorkeepers of equality. In other words, our modes of expression—the kind of language we use, its tone, cadence, and appearance—carry ethical weight in that they count as systems of control that qualify access to the institutions of power in our political systems. A poetics of political thinking, then, is attuned to the normative dimension of the technologies of evaluation—of reading and writing competence—that govern political participation.

This culture of evaluation is as vibrant in contemporary political theory as it is in popular culture writ large. If there is one thing that characterizes the tensions between the various proponents of the liberal/poststructural debate, it is the question of theoretical literacy for political evaluation: the contest is one over the standards of textual appraisal, where *textual* refers expansively to the (mis)use of words in political argument. "The issue," as Bonnie Honig rightly points out in her discussion of the genres of democracy, "is the normative import of our reading practices as political theorists and as citizens and residents of democratic regimes."[22]

The moral image of thought that governs the reading and writing practices of political argument grants de facto authority to modes of political thinking that justify claims through epistemological verification. There is a four-fold grammar to theoretical literacy that lends credence to the norms of this moral image of thought. First and foremost, legitimate political action belongs to the domain of morality, which means that it must correspond to a conception of rightness; second, philosophical justification is the language game of political action; third, in order to determine the rightness of an act, it must be justified by relying on epistemological standards of theoretical validity that determine the legitimacy of that act; finally, whether the action is performed or not is irrelevant to the telos of theoretical reflection, which is the specification of the rules of action.

Consider, as an example of the ubiquity of this moral image of thought in theoretical literacy, Martha Nussbaum's 1999 critique of Judith Butler's intellectual enterprise. The "implied reader" of a Butler essay, Nussbaum asserts, "is expected not to care greatly about Butler's own final view on many matters. For a large proportion of the sentences in any book by Butler—especially sentences near the end of chapters—are questions. Sometimes the answer that the question expects is evident. But often things are much more indeterminate ... Mystification as well as hierarchy are the tools of her practice, a mystification that eludes criticism because it makes few definite claims."[23] Nussbaum starts with the idea that ethical writing should always be didactic, beginning with questions and ending with answers in the form of "definite claims." This limits the possibility of mistaken interpretations and, indeed, of mystification and hierarchy. What some freshmen writing handbooks refer to as a "classical style" should be the dominant genre for the exposition of ethical thought.[24] Nussbaum also celebrates this vocational sentiment in the first sentence of her *Love's Knowledge*: "How should one write," she asks, "what words should one select, what forms and structures and organizations, if one is pursuing understanding? (Which is to say, if one is, in that sense, a philosopher?)."[25] Refusing to pose the problem of an ethics of the question, Nussbaum assumes that thinking should be oriented toward understanding, and that it begins with a desire and commitment to solving problems. Thus, rather than ending with questions, she begins with them, leading her reader to believe that she will provide answers. But in her litany, several questions remain unasked: What is "the sense" that characterizes the philosopher? Nussbaum criticizes Butler's philosophical and political incorrectness—an argument that, when pushed to its polemical extreme, amounts to the Socratic charge of sophistry. But is Nussbaum's sense of philosophical writing the same as Butler's sense of political writing? Or even political philosophical writing? Though they are inscribed between the lines of her polemic, Nussbaum never responds to such questions.

From Nussbaum's perspective, an ethics of theoretical literacy includes a commitment to allegory as the shape that theoretical argument should take: a theoretical argument, like a *c.s.i.* episode where the forensic facts tell the story of the crime, should be factual (rather than speculative), with a beginning, middle, and an end. The question at the beginning of a work of theory poses the problem that needs to be resolved, and the task of the writer is to adequately address that question throughout the work and generate a cogent answer at the conclusion. Moreover, when reading theoretical writing, one must search for the moral of the story, so to speak, which is to be found not in the stylistics or form of the exposition but in the content of the work itself. Thus it is Butler's choice of style that is actually condemned by Nussbaum, rather than the apparently obscure content of her writing.[26] Or rather, paraphrasing Plato's aesthetics once again, an inappropriate style obfuscates the content, thereby confusing the reader rather than clarifying an argument. The norms of theoretical literacy dictate that when either reading or writing we must avoid at any cost placing ourselves in a zone of indiscernability that impedes judgment.

This standard is invoked not only in Nussbaum's critique of Butler, but in her critique of literary theory more generally. What Nussbaum shares with the literary theorists she takes to task is the idea that the emotions can play a productive role in our moral reflections, or what she calls "perceptive equilibrium." Offering her reader a defense of the novel as a possible source for ethical insight, she shows how Henry James's *The Golden Bowl* is an exemplary discussion of certain important moral topics, not the least of which is the relevance of aesthetics to human flourishing. *The Golden Bowl* thus offers us "views very seldom examined in works of moral philosophy"; it is a text "which displays to us the complexity, the indeterminacy, the sheer *difficulty* of moral choice" that offers us "candidates for moral truth which the plainness of traditional moral philosophy lacks the power to express, and which *The Golden Bowl* expresses wonderfully."[27] In short, as she states in another work of the same period, "part of the idea of flourishing is a deep respect for qualitative difference . . . the novel, so different from a guidebook or even an anthropological field report, makes readers participants in the lives of people very different from themselves and also critics of the class distinctions that give people similarly constructed an unequal access to flourishing."[28] The exemplarity of the novel (and James's novels in particular) as a source for moral reflection lies in its ability to create counterfactual worlds that, through allegory, illustrate potential forms of living other than the ones immediately available to any reader. This, in short, is the ethical power of fiction that "the plainness" of traditional texts in moral philosophy can't live up to.

The work that Nussbaum would like the novel (and aesthetics more generally) to do is substitutive: it should stand in for the lacunae of the moral imagination. Aesthetics, on her view, is the handmaiden of moral philosophy that assists in addressing those normative issues with which the latter enterprise struggles. The ethical value of aesthetics that contemporary literary theorists like Judith Butler and Jacques Derrida (in particular)[29] overlook is the fact that "fancy" or "the metaphorical imagination"[30] can provide us with better examples of moral complexity, indeterminacy and "the sheer *difficulty* of moral choice," than can the philosopher's example and that these better examples are useful because they can help shoulder the demands of clarity.

Nussbaum's commitment to an ideology of allegory betrays an impoverished sense of value; ethical, aesthetic, or otherwise.[31] Nussbaum criticizes literary theorists for being insufficiently ethical in their concerns because, as her admonitions to Judith Butler clearly evince, she doesn't recognize the kinds of questions being posed to literary texts by literary theorists as ethical questions. By placing novels in the service of moral philosophy, she wants the literary to perform the kind of didactic work that she imagines is the purview of moral philosophy. Furthermore, the kinds of novels Nussbaum reads, the kinds she finds ethically useful, are "exemplary" (as she says) not only of the moral questions they pose but also of a style of writing that one habituated by reading analytic philosophy can recognize as being morally relevant because of their concern with questions of practical philosophy.

"It is plainly an error in a critic," David Hume remarks in *Of the Standard of Taste*, "to confine his approbation to one species or style of writing, and condemn all the rest."[32] Analogously, we might say that it is plainly an error in a moral theorist to confine approbation to one ethical style and to condemn all the rest. Our understandings of the complexity of moral life can, indeed, be enriched by aesthetic experience. But this commitment to human flourishing, to an Aristotelian *eudaimonia*, should not circumscribe what kinds of ethical experiences count as valid. An ethics of aesthetics, in other words, should not simply seek to enrich our moral imagination by providing better examples of complexity. An ethics of aesthetics can also provide an enriched account of what is available to ethical experience because, as Ian Hunter explains, aesthetics "is the means by which individuals undertake a special kind of ethical work on the being whose incompleteness they have accepted as their own."[33]

For Gilles Deleuze, for instance, writing (and literature) moves "in the direction of the ill-formed or the incomplete . . . and goes beyond the matter of any livable or lived experience."[34] The ethical force of the aesthetic resides in its flirtations with the question of becoming, which does not pursue form (through either identification, imitation, or mimesis) "but finds a zone of proximity, indiscernability, or indifferentiation." Echoing this sentiment, Michel Foucault shows how writing and transgression are intimately related. Reading and writing always imply an experience with transgression that stands as the source of all ethical experience. Transgression and the limit are in constant play with one another; "transgression incessantly crosses and recrosses a line which closes up behind it in a wave of extremely short duration, and thus it is made to return once more right to the horizon of the uncrossable."[35] Aesthetic experience, then, is ethical experience that involves an encounter with a horizon of radical alterity,[36] which is to say that aesthetic experience presupposes an ethics of difference that is not easily reducible to Nussbaum's "qualitative difference."

For Nussbaum, issues of transgression, becoming, and "fusions of horizons" might be mystifying terms that complicate rather than simplify matters. Nonetheless, this does not make such approaches to aesthetics any less ethical. They presuppose that reading and writing are first and foremost ethical activities that involve questions of authorial intention, subjectivity, and power. Nussbaum's attempt to circumscribe what counts as ethical experience in reading and writing, we are left to conclude, is the inevitable result of an uncritical reading habit that, though apparently appreciative of the complexity of ethical life, disregards the amphibology of ethical thinking.

A poetics of political thinking explores the ethics of representation from both an aesthetic and a political point of view. When discussing just political arrangements, political thinkers not only address the normative dimensions of political representation but also use compositional techniques to represent their images of political thought. Each of the following chapters is a study of the images of political thought that source contemporary accounts of the nature of political argument. I look to selected writings of Thomas Hobbes, John Rawls, Gilles Deleuze, Jürgen Habermas, Jacques Rancière, William Hazlitt, and others, with an eye to what ethical and aesthetic standards political theorists require of individuals when asked to think politically. I examine these theorists' techniques of representation vis-à-vis thinking and consider how their standards of appraisal inform their contending conceptions of political participation and action.

This book is divided into four chapters. The first, "Delicate Discriminations: Thomas Hobbes's Science of Politics," intervenes in the current debate regarding Hobbes's relation to Renaissance humanism. The rise and development of a science of politics in the seventeenth and eighteenth centuries was an attempt to regulate the flow of disparate opinions through mechanisms of translation that transformed opinion into knowledge. Hobbes participated in this general enterprise but was also keenly aware of the hermeneutic hazards it involved. By focusing on Hobbes's experiments in optics (within the Mersenne circle) and the trompe-l'oeil artistic heritage of these experiments, I show how Hobbes could not have been the kind of nominalist many historians of political thought make him out to be. I also argue that the cold war image of Hobbes as a proponent of a state-centered conception of political power is equally misguided: it overlooks the aesthetic dimensions of "representation" (a term that Hobbes infamously introduces in *Leviathan*, chapter 16) that, for someone writing in the seventeenth century, could not be distinguished from an account of "political representation." Hobbes's persistent use of the theater metaphor exemplifies a twin aesthetic and political dimension to representation suggesting that citizens do not stop representing once they consent to a sovereign. Rather, as the frontispiece Hobbes designed for *Leviathan* suggests, the sovereign is perpetually visible and hence subject to the spectator's ongoing discrimination and evaluation. In this regard, the sovereign is as much a subject of the citizen's opinion as she is a centripetal force guaranteeing stability; and, as an object of evaluation, the sovereign occasions the perpetual production and circulation of opinions rather than merely unifying individual wills into a coherent and stable whole.

Both Gilles Deleuze and Thomas Hobbes recognize the intensive force of difference in political life. For Hobbes, this occurs through his adoption of discrimination as a guiding principle of judgment and his commitment to anamorphosis as a source of political knowledge. Deleuze is equally committed to a positive conception of difference, elucidating a model of critique weary of dialectical reasoning. In my second chapter, "The Banality of the Negative: Gilles Deleuze's Ethics of the Problem," I expand on Deleuze's claim regarding philosophy's "confusion of difference with negation."[37] Deleuze explains how a problem arises in dialectical thinking regarding the relationship of identity/difference where difference is said to oppose and negate identity. The different is subsumed into a system of similitudes, and verisimilitude becomes the privileged mode of relating objects. As a possible alternative to the ethical dilemmas posed by dialectical reasoning, I discuss Deleuze's treatment of an "ethics of the question" and its relation to medieval theological writings (especially those of Duns Scotus) that represent "the negative" positively, as the site of an abundant multiplicity. I conclude by suggesting that contemporary political thinkers might find positive ethical sustenance in these critical commitments and that Deleuze's critique of negation and his articulation of an "ethics of the problem" offers valuable insights for our current understandings of foreignness, citizenship, and the value of political criticism.

Chapter 3, "The Beautiful and the Sublime in Rawls and Rancière," analyzes the poetics of liberalism and poststructuralism. Beginning with a discussion of Kantian aesthetics and the question Kant poses in the *Critique of Judgment*—namely, What kind of interest is there in objects of beauty?—I turn to John Rawls's writings and show how his project of political liberalism is indebted to the Kantian beautiful and to the creation of a political system governed by an ideal of justice defined in terms of two central aesthetic principles: mimetic representation and narrative continuity. From here, I turn to a discussion of Jacques Rancière's democratic politics of disagreement. I argue that Rancière reserves the name "democracy" for those moments when there is an interruption in the ordered composition of a social system. I conclude that, like Rawls, Rancière also relies on certain aesthetic principles. Most notably, Rancière's image of political thought is indebted to a Burkean account of the sublime. Finally, I position Rawls and Rancière to stand as exemplars of the liberal/poststructural debate in contemporary political thought in order to illustrate how contemporary debates into the nature of political argument are sourced by aesthetic standards of evaluation.

In the final chapter, "The Force of Political Argument: Habermas, Hazlitt, and the Essay," I examine the tensions that emerge between the practice of essay writing and a commitment to philosophical justification as the model for political argument. The performative contradiction is the prevalent tool of political argument and its principal value is polemical, outlining the parameters of what counts as a "good" or "bad" thought. That is, the moral prerogative of the performative contradiction wants to protect, in thought, an absolute value of the good image. There is thus a kind of policing function at work that circumscribes the form of political claims. The a priori insistence that one's utterances always be coherent is more than an attempt to rationalize political discourse; it stands as a condition of sincerity that restricts available forms of democratic action. I discuss Habermas's grounding of his critical ideal in the bourgeois public sphere and show the limits of this conception of democratic citizenship by soliciting evidence from William Hazlitt's essays. If we can characterize democracies as the persistent simultaneity of coexisting dissimilars, then the negative valuation and outright rejection of contradiction as a cognitive mistake puts pressure on the liberal democratic commitment to equality. I conclude that the simultaneously disruptive and innovative potential found in such limits as contradictions, contraries, and other anomalies comprises the challenge to contemporary political thought.

1

Delicate Discriminations

THOMAS HOBBES'S SCIENCE OF POLITICS

> We have reason to fear that the multitude of books which grows every day in a prodigious fashion will make the following centuries fall into a state as barbarous as that of the centuries that followed the fall of the Roman Empire. Unless we try to prevent this danger by separating those books which we must throw or leave in oblivion from those which one should save and, within the latter, between the parts that are useful and those which are not. —ADRIEN BAILLET

> All enlightened men seemed to be convinced that complete freedom and exemption from any form of censorship should be granted to longer works. Because writing them requires time, purchasing them requires affluence, and reading them requires attention, they are not able to produce the reaction in the populace that one fears of works of greater rapidity and violence. But *pamphlets*, and *handbills*, and *newspapers*, are produced quickly, you can buy them for little, and because their effect is immediate, they are believed to be more dangerous.
> —BENJAMIN CONSTANT

An Excess of Words

The fluidity and speed with which words travel in such public forms of writing as pamphlets, handbills, and newspapers is often considered a threat to the stability of a polity. "By the second half of the seventeenth century," Ann Blair notes, "the sense of crisis due to information overload had reached such proportions that printing, long praised as a 'divine' invention, had to be defended against the charge of bringing on a new era of barbarity."[1] This fear of barbarity, intensified by the circulation of impolitic words and even more impolitic writings, is a sentiment shared by many figures from the seventeenth through to the nineteenth centuries and, indeed, even today.[2] Whether couched in debates over literary canon formation,[3] or contests over "poor writing" in academic journals and the popular media, the fear is that the misuse of words will corrupt our ability to judge properly. Constant's characterization of longer works able to sustain a reader's attention is contrasted with a popular disdain for pamphlets, handbills, and newspapers that occasion rapid and nonreflective judgments. In the hands of the wrong people—which is to say in the hands of the people at large—such literature inevitably produces instability and dissent.

Jacques Rancière refers to this phenomenon as "the scene of the modern revolution, the revolution of the children of the Book."[4] Coinciding with the democratic revolutions of the seventeenth and eighteenth centuries, this literary revolution places great emphasis on judgment as a mode of political thinking and points to the emergence of public opinion as a legitimate form of political knowledge. In order to have knowledge, one must have correct opinions, or at least opinions not founded upon mistaken judgments. It becomes necessary, then, to invent and put into practice a series of institutional mechanisms that allow people to opine correctly. These mechanisms—like a literary canon—function to guarantee knowledge of other interlocutors; that is, by knowing how to read and knowing that others read as we do, we have access to an other's persona, allowing us to engage in (to use modern parlance) intersubjective communication.[5]

The problem of the relationship between opinion and knowledge is the central problem Thomas Hobbes tackles in his *Leviathan*, and for him this is explicitly a problem of reading competence. Consider his introduction:

> But there is another saying not of late understood . . . *Nosce teipsum, Read thy self*: which was not meant, as it is now used, to countenance, either the barbarous state of men in power, towards their inferiors: or to encourage men of low degree, to a sawcie behaviour towards their betters; But to teach us, that for the similitude of the thoughts, and Passions of one man, to the thoughts and Passions of another, whosoever looketh into himself, and considereth what he doth, when he does *think, opine, reason, hope, feare*, &c, and upon what grounds; he shall thereby read and know, what are the thoughts, and Passions, of all other men, upon the like occasions.[6]

Like Baillet, Hobbes invokes the metaphor of "barbarity" to predict the consequences of an incompetent reading public. But rather than concluding from this that barbarism produces a multiplicity of meanings, Hobbes makes barbarism an agent of the collapse of meaning. The "barbarous state" that results from the *nosce teipsum* is thus not "another" language but rather a place of nonlanguage. Reminiscent, as it is, of his infamous description of the state of nature in *Leviathan* (chapter 13), this account of the collapse of meaning emphasizes Hobbes's fear that such a barbarous state is a potential threat to the stability of any political system.

There is also a curious and noteworthy mistranslation: Hobbes translates the Latin *nosce teipsum* as "read thy self," when the more appropriate translation is "know thy self" and is recognizably the Latin translation of the Greek dictum of Apollo's oracle at Delphi.[7] The Latin verb *nosce* is the second person singular present tense of the transitive verb *noscere* (third declension—*nosco/noscis/novi/notum*), which literally means "to know" and is the root of our English *cognize* and *recognize* (it also forms the root of the French *connaître* and the Italian *conoscere*). Hobbes's mistranslation is curious particularly because we know, from accounts of his humanist education, that he was a renowned classicist fluent in both Latin and ancient Greek, along with modern French and Italian. Given this, it can only be the case that Hobbes intended to replace "to know" with "to read," and that he did so for certain specific reasons. One reason is the one he states: namely, that the expression *nosce teipsum* is being misused so as to allow people the liberty to claim a general knowledge about how things are from the position of their solitary self. Another possible reason complicates Hobbes's stature in the canon of political thought: it might be the case that Hobbes's political "subject" is as much a reading subject as a "subject of rights."

The rise and development of a modern science of politics in the seventeenth and eighteenth centuries was an attempt to regulate the flow of opinion by inventing various mechanisms of translation that transformed barbarous opinion into politically relevant knowledge. In this chapter, I reexamine Hobbes's appropriation and use of the term *representation* in political discourse. Today, we recognize and are bombarded by transubstantiating devices of representation such as the opinion poll or the advice of the political consultant—a professional persona invented to make sense of the "information overload" that opinion polls generate. Thomas Hobbes did not have the luxury of public opinion polls, or the kinds of pie graphs and flow charts found in any issue of *USA Today*. Nonetheless, the proliferation of nonauthorized opinion was a real problem for him—indeed, it is *the* problem addressed in *Leviathan*. Surrounded by the excesses of the English Civil War and faced with such barbarous speech as that of Gerard Winstanley, William Walwyn, Abeizer Coppe, and others, Hobbes saw it fit to invent a device that would convert opinion into knowledge. This invention comes in the form of a *con-science*: a kind of political knowledge that invites an aesthetic language of "representation" into a uniquely modern political vocabulary. Because Hobbes grants the individual the power to form representations through imagination and artifice, he makes room for these representations to count as something other than mere images. In other words, Hobbes admits that there can be no natural laws of "truth" governing a polity; this is why his polity is, importantly, *artificial*. It thus becomes critical that citizens formulate representations and solicit approval of them from others, thereby creating something like a common public opinion. On this rendering, the practice of representation and the solicitation of approval through judgment become the cornerstones of consent.

I place great emphasis on several features of Hobbes's argument and, indeed, on the figure of Hobbes himself. I first consider a question that has, as of yet, not been adequately pursued: what would it mean for such a committed nominalist as Hobbes to also be a polyglot?[8] The entirety of book 1 of *Leviathan*, ending with the crucial chapter (16) on representation, is typically characterized as a discussion of the right use of words. In this regard, many scholars note that Hobbes is a nominalist who devises a science of politics.[9] But Thomas Hobbes was also someone who spoke more than four languages fluently and spent a substantial amount of energy pursuing translations of ancient texts (the most famous of these being his classic translation of Thucydides's *The Peloponnesian War*). My point is that discussions of Hobbes's nominalism must account for his ability to call any one thing by several names. The fact that Hobbes's polyglot education made him aware of the multilingual character within any particular language complicates his relationship to the nominalist outlook conventionally attributed to him. Or, to put the matter differently, Hobbes reverts to and endorses nominalism as one would, in our day, revert to and endorse the device of the opinion poll: nominalism is a *techne*—a device of representation—that functions to halt the flow of barbarous speech.[10] Hobbes's nominalism, then, does not consist in a rejection of universals per se but instead lies in the affirmation of particulars. Though concepts may be general and universal, their manifestation in the world is the result of particular judgments, and the choices resultant from individual discriminations are of immediate political import.

Conventional readings of Hobbes present him as proffering a theory of government that relies on coercion as the principal guarantor of legitimacy. By looking at his conceptions of power, freedom, and the role of political representation therein, readers of Hobbes insist that his is a frightening vision, potentially leading to unspeakable excesses of power. Admittedly, there is ample textual evidence for such a reading, especially when reading Hobbes in the midst of the kind of political climate that the cold war occasioned. Archetypal instances of such symptomatic misreadings include the following:

> Liberalism does not in principle have to depend on specific religious or philosophical systems of thought. It does not have to choose among them as long as they do not reject toleration, which is why Hobbes is not the father of liberalism. No theory that gives public authorities the unconditional right to impose beliefs and even a vocabulary as they may see fit upon the citizenry can be described as even remotely liberal. Of all the cases made against liberalism, the most bizarre is that liberals are really indifferent, if not openly hostile, to personal freedom. This may follow from the peculiar identification of *Leviathan* as the very archetype of liberal philosophy, but it is a truly gross misinterpretation which simply assures that any social contract theory, however authoritarian its intentions, and any anti-Catholic polemic add up to liberalism. (Judith Shklar)[11]

> Hobbes, and those who agreed with him, especially conservative or reactionary thinkers, argued that if men were to be prevented from destroying one another and making social life a jungle or a wilderness, greater safeguards must be instituted to keep them in their places; he wished correspondingly to increase the area of centralized control and decrease that of the individual. (Isaiah Berlin)[12]

In each case, Hobbes's "contract" is a sacrificial act where citizens give up their liberties for the greater good of social and political stability. Shklar's "liberalism of fear" impugns Hobbes with a version of totalitarianism, and Berlin's classic description of Hobbes, though sympathetic to his concept of "negative liberty," is equally disturbed by the presence of absolutism. To be sure, it is not that these positions are inchoate, but rather that their cogency rests on a reading strategy that relies on an absolutist architectonic of power. But such a conception of power seems inappropriate given that Hobbes's metaphysics is more complex than the architectonic metaphor allows.[13] These symptomatic misreadings of Hobbes are symptomatic principally as a consequence of an equally misbegotten reading strategy: one that eschews the at once aesthetic and, indeed, poetical dimensions of Hobbes's political thought.[14]

In his day, Hobbes was renowned not only for his philosophical rigor but, most vividly, for his command of style and rhetoric, and it was the combination of poetic language with powerful ideas that made him both famous and infamous.[15] In light of this, Hanna Pitkin's assertion that "Hobbes' discussion of representation is confined almost entirely to chapter 16 of his major work, *Leviathan. Thus the context is one of political rather than, say, esthetic thought*," is curious, to say the least.[16] Why is the context political and not aesthetic? Or rather, what is at stake in distinguishing between these two modes of thinking? Given Hobbes's influential defense of discrimination as the quintessential faculty for judging representations, could it not be the case that the political and the aesthetic are intimately related in his treatment of representation? In emphasizing the poetic dimension of representation, I hope to show that there is a substantive aesthetic component to Hobbes's political thinking that cannot be easily separated from matters of political import. Indeed, the representational mechanism Hobbes devises brings out the aesthetic and political richness of his artistic innovations for thinking through a science of politics.

Thomas Hobbes in Translation

> If I am not mistaken, the distinguishing character of Lucretius (I mean his soul and genius) is a certain kind of noble pride, and positive assertion of his opinion. . . . From his time to ours, I know none so like him, as our poet and philosopher of Malmesbury. —JOHN DRYDEN

Much has been made of Thomas Hobbes's relationship to Renaissance humanism. The growing literature—which includes such immediately notable scholars as David Johnston, Victoria Kahn, Noel Malcolm, Quentin Skinner, Nancy Struever, Richard Tuck, and others—inaugurates what might best be described as a historiographical revision of Hobbes's stature within the canon of political thought. The writerly Hobbes, as Michael Oakeshott describes him, is "a self-conscious stylist" whose idea of thinking "was not only conceived as movement, it was felt as movement."[17] Hobbes's concern for style is characteristic of his writings in general; he was indeed someone who *used* arguments as much as he was an expositor of a philosophical outlook and, as one scholar notes, his "fascination with the axiomatic method and its explanatory potential did not in any sense constitute a rejection of the rhetorical tradition that had shaped Hobbes's thinking during the first forty years of his life."[18] Conventional readings of Hobbes criticize his apparent insistence that the relationship between signifier and signified is fixed and that this fixing is coercively imposed by the sovereign.[19] He is further criticized for at once attacking the use of ornate language and littering his own *Leviathan* with metaphors of all sorts. Indeed, the title of the work is a metaphor intended to describe the body politic. Quentin Skinner has argued that such "unwisely condescending accusations" are mistaken, because "what these critics fail to register is the degree to which Hobbes's use of *ornatus* in *Leviathan* mirrors a new-found willingness to endorse a humanist understanding of the proper relationship between reason and eloquence."[20]

Skinner is right to signal what these facile criticisms overlook, but one wonders whether Hobbes's willingness to endorse *ornatus* is, in fact, "new-found." Skinner's account marks *Leviathan* as the apotheosis of the Hobbesian corpus; in it we find a synthesis of aesthetic, political, and philosophical language underscoring Hobbes's commitment to Renaissance humanism, once overshadowed by his more "scientific" writings (especially *The Elements of Law*).[21] But to put the matter thus seems to miss the point of Hobbes's persistent fascination with the workings of language. For instance, Hobbes's interest in translating Thucydides's *The Peloponnesian Wars* is not merely an instance of his early humanist writings, as Skinner portrays it, but also marks the beginning of a more general interest in the study of optics and perspectivism. Hobbes exploits this curiosity with perspectivism—with a kind of "looking awry"—in his optical experiments with the Mersenne circle which go a long way in explaining his complex account of representation. For Hobbes, translation is the linguistic corollary to perspectivism, and both are crucial to his understanding of a science of politics. To clarify: It is not that we arrive at the correct meaning of an object by "looking awry," as if there were a proper perspective from which to judge the legitimacy of representations. Rather, Hobbes's appreciation of the complexities of translation suggests that each position whence we may have a perspective is skewed from the perspective of every other position. Allow me to expand on this point with an example from the world of painting.

At first glance, Hans Holbein the Younger's *The Ambassadors* (1533) seems like a conventional portrait. In fact, we know that the occasion for its inception was to commemorate the arrival in England of Georges de Selve (Bishop of Lavour), who was visiting his friend Jean de Dinteville, the French envoy in London. It was one of the first major works Holbein painted after his decision in 1532 to settle permanently in England, and it remains the most recognizable of the artist's oeuvre. De Dinteville's presence in England coincided with Henry VIII's secret marriage to Anne Boleyn (followed by her coronation), and it is speculated that de Selve's visit was intended to suggest to the English monarchy that the papacy would look favorably on Henry's marriage to Anne.[22] From this, one might correctly deduce that *The Ambassadors* is a painting born of political controversy, in the midst of what John Rawls refers to as "the historical origin of political liberalism."[23] More important for our immediate interests, however, is the painting itself.

The two French ambassadors stand next to some shelves draped with fine cloths. The floor upon which they stand is a reproduction of the inlaid marble mosaic of Westminster Abbey. Between them, scattered haphazardly on the shelves, is a cluster of objects that includes a lute with a missing string (signifying discord), a celestial globe, astronomical instruments, books (one of which is a hymnal open to Martin Luther's "Chorale"), a sundial, compasses, and what has been described as "a strange object, like a cuttle-fish bone" that floats above the floor.[24] I will return to this strange object shortly. For now, it is worth remarking that the collection of Renaissance artifacts separating the two figures seems awkward, given that the painting is intended as a portrait and, in fact, they make it seem as though the two figures are objects of the still life rather than subjects of the study.

The objects organized on the shelves, though seemingly disparate,

FIGURE 1: Hans Holbein the Younger, *Jean de Dinteville and Georges de Selve* (*The Ambassadors*). © The National Gallery, London. Reprinted with permission.

are symbolically relevant and interconnected. A sixteenth-century audience would have immediately recognized these as symbols of Renaissance humanism. One art historian explains how, "through these symbolic forms, bearing the stamp of Italy, Holbein is in direct contact with certain books and even certain images, with the original reasoning behind them, and first and foremost, with *The Praise of Folly*, the work of Erasmus of Rotterdam, his friend and patron."[25]

The connection between Erasmus and Holbein goes a long way in helping us understand *The Ambassadors*. In *The Praise of Folly* Erasmus famously enlarges on the theme of the vanity of knowledge — a theme readily available to Renaissance scholars, from Thomas More to Sebastian Brant and Cornelius Agrippa. Instead of glorifying the sciences, these authors typically ridiculed learning by focusing their attention on how the senses deceive the mind. The portrayal of knowledge as worthy of jest and laughter relies on perspectivism as the means by which one cultivates learning. The potential that all perception is skewed perception, implicit in the idea of perspectivism, invokes a comical stance vis-à-vis the production of knowledge. Agrippa, for instance, in *The Declamation on the Uncertainty, vanity and abuses of the Sciences and the Arts*, privileges optics (synonymous with perspective) as a style of learning, ranking it immediately after geometry so that "perspective [becomes] one of the geometrical measures of the world."[26] But this measure is also, and in all respects, a hoax. By conjoining geometry with perspectivism, the vanities of knowledge are revealed.

In this environment of scientific hoaxes and political follies, Holbein's *The Ambassadors* becomes an allegorical representation of the intersection between the vanity of knowledge and the vanity of terrestrial power. Separated by the symbols of Renaissance learning, the two French emissaries are comical figures not only because of their apparent learnedness (as exemplified in the seriousness of their expressions), but also for the earthly power they pretend to wield. Significant for this reading of the work is the "cuttle-fish figure" that hovers before them. From a frontal perspective, it is an awkward object that seems to have nothing to do with the painting: it is the one object that is not immediately recognizable. But the painting is not as literal as it appears; that is, the painting is more than an allegorical portrait (although it is also just that). Holbein gave precise instructions for the hanging of the painting: "It had to be placed at the base of a wall, on a level with or slightly above the floor, which would seem to extend into the picture."[27] But when we imagine a door at either end of the wall on which the painting hangs, and we exit the room from the door on the right, we are given immediate—though brief—access to the "cuttle-fish figure."[28] From this perspective, at the instant when we are about to leave the room, we realize that the figure is a skull and—in a moment that has been likened to ideological demystification[29]—we realize further that the allegorical painting of the two French emissaries, their objects, and the Westminster mosaic upon which they stand is, in fact, a painting that ridicules the convergence of the kind of intellectual and political power that the frontal perspective invokes. The integrity of the painting, held together by the seemingly nonsensical element that hovers in the foreground, is dissolved by that same element. This trompe-l'oeil effect is called anamorphosis, and it is one of the more important sites of inquiry for the study of optics and perspective in the sixteenth and seventeenth centuries. In this regard, Holbein's *The Ambassadors* may be read as an instance of Erasmian "folly." The anamorphic moment in the painting offers an experience of an illusory reality that is as real as real can get. This moment does not make the painting meaningless, nor does it suggest that the previous perspective was mistaken. Rather, it shifts the register of meaning from an exaggerated realism to a humorous tone of perspective gone awry. "The skull is a non-place," notes Stephen Greenblatt. "But to enter this non-place is to alter everything in the painting and to render impossible a simple return to normal vision."[30] The optical perspective of anamorphosis transforms the painting from a drama of political and scholarly excellence to a comedy of sorts. It is, in short, at least two different kinds of paintings in one.[31] On this reading, Holbein's *The Ambassadors* is analogous to Hobbes's conception of perspective in language and politics.

It is by now commonplace to include, in discussions of the writerly Hobbes, an account of his membership in the Mersenne circle while in Paris writing *Leviathan*.[32] We also know that Marin Mersenne, an ascetic monk of the Minime order, gave particular importance to anamorphosis and was, like Holbein, steeped in the tradition of jest exemplified in Erasmus's and Agrippa's works. So much so, in fact, that Mersenne's principal work (*Universal Harmony*, 1636) may be read as a commentary on the vanities of knowledge and terrestrial power as it "allows us to see how the realization of the vanities and follies of human sciences leads directly to philosophic doubt. In the process, by describing their nature, it forms a link with the experiments on deception in the realm of pure optics which were being assiduously carried out."[33] Thus in the midst of the production of what Skinner refers to as Hobbes's "scientific writings" we see the relevance of anamorphosis to Hobbes's thinking.

Hobbes's own concern with deception in optics is a corollary to his fear of barbarism: a concern, I submit, stemming from his polyglotism. While writing *The Elements of Law*, Hobbes was also working on a study of optics (*Tractatus opticus*). Richard Tuck suggests that Hobbes's interest in optics was primarily epistemological: it was a curiosity shared by the members of the Mersenne circle more generally and was encouraged by encounters with the works of Galileo and, perhaps, by encounters with Galileo himself. The latter's approach was particularly appealing to these "post-skeptics" "because it stressed the non-straightforward character of physical observation."[34] This interest in perspectivism is especially evident in Hobbes's complicated discussion of the nature of moral philosophy in *Leviathan*. Echoing Galileo's belief in the objectivity of nature's laws, Hobbes insists that "the laws of nature are immutable and eternal."[35] However, knowledge of these laws—that is, moral philosophy—requires an investigation into "what is good and evil in the conversation and society of mankind." And further,

> Good and evil are names that signify our appetites and aversions, which in different tempers, customs, and doctrines of men are different; and diverse men differ not only in their judgment on the senses of what is pleasant and unpleasant to the taste, smell, hearing, touch, and sight but also of what is conformable or disagreeable to reason in the actions of common life. Nay, the same man in divers times differs from himself, and one time praises—that is, calls good—what another time

he dispraises and calls evil; from whence arise disputes, controversies, and at last war.[36]

Judgment, in other words, is of the order of particularities grounded in individual experience. Though the laws of nature are immutable, their application in human life is the result of differing conceptions of good and evil, so that though concepts of nature persist through time, the particularity of our experience of them differs precisely because of our perspective in discrimination. The point, then, is to note a substantive distinction Hobbes makes between a science of nature and a science of politics: while the former deals with universals, the latter concerns the appraisal of particulars that is necessarily political (that is, it sources our disputes, controversies and, ultimately, war).

The epistemological and aesthetic implications of anamorphosis also have repercussions for Hobbes's penchant for translation.[37] In the preface to his translation of Thucydides, Hobbes contests previous translations of the work. He proudly asserts that his translation, which "lay long by [him]" before he chose to "communicate" it to the world, is better than the ones available since his comes from the original Greek text. Previous translations follow the Latin version of Laurentius Valla, "which was not without some errors; and he, a Greek copy not so correct as now is extant."[38] From there it was translated into French, and from the French into English, and so, "as by multiplication of error [Thucydides] became at length traduced, rather than translated into our language."[39] The difference between traducing and translating amounts to the difference between a bad and a good copy of the work. But here, the apparent slippage into what today might be called a "metaphysics of origins" is halted by Hobbes's description of how he approached the task of translation: "Hereupon," he asserts, "I resolved to take him [Thucydides] immediately from the Greek, according to the edition of Æmilius Porta: *not refusing or neglecting any version, comment, or other help I could come by*."[40] As Hobbes sees it, the enterprise of translation is one that requires other judgments, voices, and opinions. Woven into the text, this constitutive multivoicedness functions as counsel for Hobbes the translator.

Hobbes insists that a good translation is a correct translation, a lucid one, and one done with elegance. He is also thoroughly aware that this enterprise is of necessity a form of "barbarism." The activity of translating is one that, by definition, involves the importation to one's domicile of what is foreign. Given this, it is not surprising to find John Dryden, in the same piece where he praises Hobbes's poetical acumen, likening translation to a disease of the mind.[41] Translation for these authors was a disease of the mind to the extent that it necessitated the possibility of occupying a foreign perspective. It thus stands as the linguistic corollary to the kind of optic anamorphosis found in Holbein's painting: Though there are a variety of perspectives whence we might view the work, such perspectives count as different only from the position of another perspective. The force of this claim resounds in the fact that to have a perspective requires the recognition of other possible perspectives coexisting with my own, just like, by practicing translation, we are forced to recognize other languages that, precisely because they are not one's own, are barbaric.

Hobbes may indeed have been a nominalist. But, as Richard Flathman rightly points out, to leave it at that misses the point of Hobbes's complex relationship to language, metaphysics, and science. The more pertinent point, then, is that Hobbes's nominalism "included an out-of-hand rejection of all 'referential' or 'object-word' theories of meaning—that is, all theories according to which the meanings of words are or could be given by reason or rationally derived from the 'things' that the words name."[42] This out-of-hand rejection, I would add, is not necessarily the result of a metaphysical deduction (although that might be part of it) but is a condition of the perspectivism at the heart of Hobbes's political thought. But if observation is inextricably linked to anamorphosis, what are we to make of Hobbes's "science of politics" and the kind of thinking it occasions? For answers we must turn to Hobbes's considerations on judgment in *Leviathan*.

A Science of Opinion

> In the first place, *barbarisms* and *solecisms* must not be allowed to intrude their offensive presence. These blemishes are however pardoned at times, because we have become accustomed to them or because they have age or authority in their favor, or are near akin to positive excellences, since it is difficult to distinguish such blemishes from figures of speech. The teacher therefore, that such slippery customers may not elude detection, must seek to acquire a delicate discrimination [*discrimen*]. —QUINTILIAN

From his initial writings through to his "scientific" period and beyond, the problem of different perspectives is a persistent preoccupation for Hobbes. The polemical excursus on the *nosce teipsum* indicates his concern for the inadequacy of public opinion, not because it is an insufficient form of political knowledge but because there is no reliable mechanism that will translate it into something like a knowledge of political life. Given the proliferation of political agents who claim authority through their private knowledge and public actions, and, further, given that these same individuals claim authoritative knowledge by the mistaken assumption that they may generalize from their own "thoughts, opinions, reasons, hopes, and fears," to the "thoughts, opinions, reasons, hopes, and fears" of others, to simply rely on these apparently "authoritative" claims without a scale by which to measure them is tantamount to self-destruction: "And though by mens actions wee do discover their designe sometimes," Hobbes explains, "yet to do it without comparing them with our own, and distinguishing all circumstances, by which the case may come to be altered, is to decypher without a key, and be for the most part deceived, by too much trust, or by too much diffidence; as he that reads, is himself a good or evil man."[43] The ability to "read" is an essential political skill and one that involves the related virtues of "distinguishing" and "comparing." In order to be a successful actor in the political arena, one must be able to distinguish one's self from the self of others and do so by comparing the differences between the varying actions of individuals. We can liken Hobbes's project in *Leviathan* to his interests in translation and anamorphosis more generally: that is, in searching for the key that might help one decipher public opinion and action, Hobbes wants to fashion a device by means of which one may translate the *nosce teipsum* into a "con-science." This device comes to us in Hobbes's appeal to representation.

Of all the works of the Hobbesian oeuvre, *Leviathan* is the first to include the term *representation*. Though many have argued that the ideas regarding the function of representation in politics were already available in his *De Cive*, Hobbes nonetheless and self-consciously shifts to an aesthetic language of representation in *Leviathan*, and he does so at a strategic moment in the text, in the very last chapter of book 1.[44] We can speculate, with Richard Tuck, that the term *representation* might be a transliteration of the French term used in Sorbière's French translation of *De Cive* (1649) and, as Tuck further speculates, it might have been Hobbes himself who suggested this term to Sorbière.[45] Thus, the singularly important achievement that, for many, situates Hobbes at the origin of a modern science of politics is the result of a double translation: on the one hand, it is a barbaric appropriation of a foreign term and on the other, it is a translation of a term from one domain of thinking (aesthetics) to another (politics).

This confluence of aesthetics and politics is immediately apparent when the reader opens the cover-leaf of *Leviathan*. There, staring up, is a representation of the experience of perspectivism in the infamous figure of the sovereign, shaped by a multitude of other bodies. We know from an anonymous French writer who wrote an article on the title page (in 1852) that, in all likelihood, "Hobbes must have devised this title-page in Paris and closely supervised its execution."[46] From the carefully tabulated imagery and the symbolic relationship these images have with the work itself, the complex figure of Leviathan "becomes a version of the traditional author-portrait in which the author and the concepts he expounds in his book are united into a single image."[47]

The frontispiece offers Hobbes's readers a first instance of representation so that his initial treatment of this concept is not in chap-

FIGURE 2: Frontispiece to Thomas Hobbes, *Leviathan* (1651). *Courtesy of Thomas Fisher Rare Book Library, University of Toronto.*

ter 16 but rather in the title page itself: The citizens comprising the body of the Leviathan are standing, facing the sovereign, with their back to the reader so that she is not privy to their expressions.[48] What she is privy to, however, is the fact that the citizens have their heads covered. This offers occasion for pause, as the rules of conduct of the period prohibited subjects from covering their heads in the presence of sovereignty so as to avoid suspicion. There are various accounts of why Hobbes might have left the citizens' heads covered: one attributes this to the engraver's "rusticity"; another suggests that Hobbes intended these people to be "insolent schismatics" and would have left their head covers on to show their defiance; yet another, equally plausible, explanation is that "the one occasion when a crowd might stand before a king without uncovering is when they are in a theater watching an actor represent the king."[49] This latter point—in conjunction with the plethora of theatrical metaphors that litter *Leviathan* and structure chapter 16—sheds much light on Hobbes's adoption of aesthetics, anamorphosis, and the metaphor of "theatrical production" for his image of sovereignty.

As I suggest, Hobbes's principal concern in *Leviathan* is to conceive of a way that the multitude of opinions and beliefs generated from an equally multitudinous populace might be designed and made recognizable. This concern with the one and the many is exploited in his use of representation and the theatrical images that account for the operation of "personating." Through their sovereign-oriented gaze the citizens generate a sense of attachment to the spectacle of sovereignty, so that "the unification of diversity follows from individuals in the audience producing the illusion which constitutes them as an audience."[50] The frontispiece of *Leviathan*—that unites both anamorphic and theatrocratic images—is a primary indication of the kind of relation of legitimation through "representation" Hobbes has in mind. The suggestion that Hobbes might have wanted the reader to "judge the book by its cover" seems difficult to deny, given that the allegorical summary that is the frontispiece occasions just that.

Judgment is, indeed, a principal topos of inquiry. But it would be too rash a conclusion to say that Hobbes understands judgment in ex-

38 CHAPTER I

clusively procedural terms. Invoking Quintilian's sense of *discrimen*, Hobbes asserts early in the book,

> Those that observe their similitudes, in case they be such as are but rarely observed by others, are sayd to have a *Good Wit*; by which, in this occasion, is meant a *Good Fancy*. But they that observe their differences, and dissimilitudes; which is called *Distinguishing*, and *Discerning*, and *Judging* between thing and thing; in case such discerning be not easy, are said to have good *Judgment*: and particularly in matter of conversation and business; wherein times, places, and persons are to be discerned, this Vertue is called *Discretion*.[51]

The ability to observe similarities and that of discerning differences are two distinct activities. The former corresponds to a good wit, the latter to good judgment; this latter talent of discretion is critical to public life.[52] This last point goes a long way in distancing Hobbes from the "symptomatic misreadings" I discussed previously. For, if Hobbes privileges the ability to discern differences between entities (that is, to discriminate) when judging, then the claim that his political philosophy is simply about the unification of wills and the elimination of differences for the sake of harmony is uninformed. To be sure, the point of the social contract is to orchestrate a multitude into some representable whole, but this whole is neither passive (pace Shklar) nor does it merely require citizens to surrender their right of participation.

Such symptomatic misreadings overlook the formal features of representation operating in Hobbes's text. By "formal features" I mean the structural components that need to be in place in order for the mechanism of representation to function. Given the specular play of gazes operating in the sovereign/subject relation, the subject's ability to create an image of the sovereign (that is, to represent a *persona ficta*) and communicate that image to others solicits evaluative judgments that then circulate publicly as would a rumor or gossip. That is, the fundamental creative ability of the subject to engender and appraise a representation of the sovereign produces a public opinion of that representation the moment it is given an audience. On this rendering, the persona ficta that is the sovereign—by the very fact of its visibility as an object of representation—is under constant public scrutiny and is persistently subject to "the censure of a multitude."[53]

Like a work of art, a literary text, or a theatrical production, the sovereign is an object that appears and circulates in public.[54] Insisting on the theatrical metaphor, Hobbes's etymology of the word *person* from the Latin *persona* is relevant:

> *Persona* in latine signifies the *disguise*, or *outward appearance* of a man, counterfeited on the Stage; and sometimes more particularly that part of it, which disguiseth the face, as a Mask or Visard: And from the Stage, hath been translated to any representer of speech and action, as well in Tribunalls, as Theatres. So that a *Person*, is the same that an *Actor* is, both on the Stage and in common Conversation; and to *Personate*, is to *Act*, or *Represent* himselfe, or another; and he that acteth another, is said to bear his Person, or act in his name.[55]

As relevant as the Latin may be, this definition notably omits its Hellenic debt to the word *hypocrite* (from the Greek meaning "the acting of a part on the stage" and, even more notably, from *hypo*, meaning "beneath," and *crisis*, meaning "judgment").[56] The one who personates another—who is said to represent an other's authority—is a hypocrite who relies on the common understanding of what it means to have a persona: namely, to have an *outward appearance subject to an other's judgment*. What is more, whenever a person acts, they are representing themselves (or another) so that the most human of all attributes—that which marks them as individual[57]—is to partake in representation.

The sovereign's outward appearance—her representational status—places her actions under the perpetual scrutiny of her audience, just like an actor's performance in a theatrical production. Rather than merely transforming humans into passive recipients of sovereign authority, Hobbes makes Quintilian's *discrimen* the critical faculty for political thinking. As a *persona ficta*, the sovereign's legitimacy is stable only as long as the public continues to recommend it. But when the Leviathan is subject to a spectator's delicate discrimination, the potential threat of legitimation crisis ensues; that is, the perpetual potential of dissolution exists because one is never sure when the frontal gaze of the spectator will shift to an anamorphic perspective. The political force of such a commitment to individual discrimination is nowhere more evident than in Hobbes's insistence that "the obligation of subjects to the sovereign is understood to last as long and no longer than the power lasts by which he is able to protect them."[58] Though Hobbes does not, himself, give particular examples of how and why this might come about, he does presume that subjects know when such a scenario might occur so that one's discriminatory competencies have such an effect as to dissolve contractual obligations.

Hans Holbein offers us a painting that compels movement. Similarly, Hobbes shows that the sovereign is a source of incompatible perspectives between which the spectator restlessly shifts.[59] This agitated shifting is not determined by the multiplicity of meanings that may or may not be available but is, rather, a condition arising from movement, which, for Hobbes, defines liberty and the natural order of things. Mobility is thus a condition of political subjectivity; hence Hobbes's negative definition of freedom as the absence of opposition, by which he means an absence of "externall Impediments of motion."[60] Liberty allows the persistence of different perspectives, and this is as true of the translator (one who moves freely between a multiplicity of languages), as it is for the viewer facing an anamorphic painting, or the citizen-spectator. In each case the shift in perspective implies an ability to discriminate.[61] Hobbes inaugurates a "science of politics" but his sense of science has very little to do with our own postnuclear understandings of it.[62] Hobbes affirms that "No Discourse whatsoever, can End in absolute knowledge of Fact, past, or to come. For, as for the knowledge of Fact, it is originally, Sense; and, ever after, Memory. And for the knowledge of Consequence, which I have said before is called Science, it is not Absolute but conditional."[63] The object and process of scientific inquiry enters into Hobbes's schema through his commitment to perspectivism and empiricism: an apprehension is given to the senses, and through imaginative reproduction it is translated into linguistic marks and held up for approval. The kind of knowledge we may have about the world is necessarily mediated by our apprehensions, which are, in themselves, perpetually subject to anamorphic distortion. The strongest sense of "certitude" we may have is limited by what we can know in common:

> When two, or more men, know of one and the same fact, they are said to be CONSCIOUS of it one to another; which is as much as to know it together. And because such are fittest witnesses of the facts of one another, or of a third; it was, and ever will be reputed a very Evil act, for any man to speak against his *Conscience*; or to corrupt or force another to do so: Insomuch that the plea of Conscience, has been always harkened unto very diligently in all times. Afterwards, men made use of the same word metaphorically, for the knowledge of their own secret facts, and secret thoughts; and therefore it is Rhetorically said that the Conscience is a thousand witnesses. And last of all, men, vehemently in love with their own opinions, (though never so absurd,) and obstinately bent to maintain them, gave those their opinions that reverenced name of Conscience, as if they would have it seem unlawful, to change or speak against them; and so pretend to know they are true, when they know at most, but that they think so.[64]

Once again, Hobbes adorns himself in classicist garb and puts into play an imprecise etymology so as to convey the sense of "knowing" he has in mind. We know that the term *conscience* is not equivalent to a con-science but rather derives from the Latin *conscientia*, which means either a privity of common knowledge or, more appropriately, a knowledge within one's self: a private knowledge. But Hobbes insists that contemporary users of the word *conscience* have forgotten its "rhetorical" origin. Originally, Hobbes narrates, conscience meant a "knowing-with-others," and it was later used metaphorically to signify a knowledge of one's own secrets, as in the expression "the conscience is a thousand witnesses." Hobbes's inventive etymology of *con-science* parallels his mistranslation of *nosce teipsum*, and both of these artifices function rhetorically to correct the misbegotten and hubristic practice of asserting one's beliefs as if they were truths, an attitude Hobbes ultimately shares with Holbein, Erasmus, Agrippa, and other expositors of the vanities of knowledge.

From this, two things become apparent: First, Hobbes's various mistranslations are intended to persuade an audience to change their beliefs and practices; that is, these mistranslations count as critical interventions into the fund of public opinions and do so by relying on an authoritative rhetoric rather than on the neutral force of the better argument. Second, Hobbes resorts to a science of politics to derive evaluative standards for public judgment. Such standards, however, do not result from a priori deductions but are products of shared opinions and shared judgments. As con-science, Hobbes's science of politics increases the production and circulation of opinion in a commonwealth, all the while attempting to translate such opinions into recognizable representations: Hobbes is committed to the production, rather than the deployability, of knowledge, meaning that his understanding of what counts as knowledge—pace Shklar, Pitkin, Wolin, and others—cannot be reduced to its functionality.[65] Thus the value of *wealth* in *commonwealth* is the production and circulation of shared opinions and representations—shared, that is, not because they are the same as everybody else's but because they are in constant circulation and subject to comparison and delicate discriminations. *Discrimen*—the ability to perceive differences—becomes the critical faculty for political thinking.

This is the aesthetico-political function of "representation" that the symptomatic misreadings of Hobbes repeatedly overlook: through his peculiar sense of con-science, Hobbes invents a mechanism that attempts to govern the play of signification within a polity but, at one and the same time, is aware of the fact that this mechanism of representation (of which "nominalism" is an instance) increases the fund and circulation of representations. Since representations are always readily available and opinions about these representations are equally readily generated, Hobbes's image of political thought transforms significations into the kinds of objects that occasion individual discrimination and, subsequently, public opinion. In short, for Hobbes there can be no individual claim to general knowledge (i.e., nosce teipsum) without it having to be sifted through the filter of public discrimination (i.e., con-science); and this general rule is as true for the sovereign as it is for the subjects of sovereignty.

The account I sketch out above can make sense only if we consider the fact that, just as Hobbes was displeased about political upheavals like the English Civil War, he was equally displeased about the possibility of perpetual stasis (something he equated with death). Indeed, his own account of "negative liberty"—an account that in part derives from his Heraclitian metaphysics—is one that promotes the perpetual motion of entities including opinions, beliefs, and persons. This poetic Hobbes imagines politics as the persistent simultaneity of co-existing dissimilars and regards political thinking as a relatively unstable practice of contrasting faculties. Consider these concluding words from *Leviathan*:

> Again, in all Deliberations, and in all Pleadings, the faculty of solid Reasoning, is necessary: for without it, the Resolutions of men are rash, and their Sentences unjust: and yet, if there be not powerful eloquence, which procureth attention and Consent, the effect of Reason will be little. But these are contrary Faculties; the former being grounded upon principals of Truth; the other upon Opinions already received, true, or false; and upon the Passions and Interests of men, which are different, and mutable.[66]

Contrary faculties indeed! Thinking, ratiocination, eloquence, and opinion are always in constant and unpredictable tension with one another, and Hobbes is ultimately undecided on which side to rest. The passage above, characteristic of his mind-set more generally, has him struggling with an ideal of certitude and a reality of cosmic flux. But this struggle is a necessary consequence of the fluid world he imagines himself to occupy. If politics—like the cosmos—is in such a turbulent state, then political thinking must be equally turbulent and perpetually fluctuating between truth and falsity, belief and opinion, passions and interests.

In this respect, Oakeshott is right to characterize Hobbes as a "master stylist" whose idea of thinking "was not only conceived as movement, it was felt as movement." Similarly, Baillet and Constant are justified in their fear of the proliferation of voices, opinions, and judgments; that is, the proliferation of the barbarity of a polity that reads. Hobbes shared this fear of reading strategies and judging practices: "There is something, I know not what," reads the first line of the preface to his translation of Thucydides, "in the censure of a multitude, more terrible than any single judgment, how severe or exact soever."[67] Public opinion—the delicate discrimination of a multitude—is, indeed, something to fear. Where this fear is unwarranted is in the assumption—held by many readers of Hobbes—that he thought something other than shifting perspectives possible in political life. There is little evidence to support the claim that Hobbes believed in the existence of such a stable entity, although he did think that recognizable representations could be devised. As he clearly states about sovereignty, "though sovereignty, in the intention of them that make it, be immortal, yet is it in its own nature not only subject to violent death by foreign war, but also through the ignorance and passions of men, it has in it, from the very institution, many seeds of a natural mortality by intestine discord."[68] His own attempt to create a mechanism that would grant us such an admittedly distorted and temporary perspective is Hobbes's greatest contribution to a modern science of politics. At the same time, Hobbes's commitment to anamorphosis attests to his equally strong belief (and hope) that a "permanent resolution" could never last forever. For him, it could last only as long as the spectator/reader had a frontal view of the representation. But the likelihood that such a perspective could shift as a result of the viewer's own movement—the potential of anamorphosis—would never be denied by our writerly Hobbes.

2

The Banality of the Negative

GILLES DELEUZE'S ETHICS OF THE PROBLEM

> "To be like myself, does this not simply mean to be like?
> I am like, but like whom? No doubt like him who, himself, is like me."
>
> "But who are we if one and the same image designates us both, even to one another?"
>
> "Resemblance is in itself treason. For it encourages the other not ever to try and know us."
>
> ". . . like nothing, the Nothing that is like nothing else, drunk with fullness, full of us, in the dimensions of the world."
>
> The foreigner? The foreign I? —EDMUND JABÈS

Jabès and the Foreigner

The above fragment from Jabès's *A Foreigner Carrying in the Crook of His Arm a Tiny Book* links foreignness to an aesthetics of resemblance and to political power. The "foreign I" is the nothing "drunk with fullness"—a paradoxical figure that contests the logic of resemblance. In these lines Jabès poses the problem of democratic pluralism—and, indeed, the problem of belonging—within the context of a philosophy of difference that, by rejecting the treasonous power of resemblance as a source of political unity, wants to imagine the possibility of foreignness as a kind of overabundant nothingness.

In this chapter I address Gilles Deleuze's central claim that critical philosophy is plagued by "the banality of the negative."[1] Echoing Jabès, Deleuze thinks that contemporary criticism is conditioned to think the concept of difference *in opposition* to the concept of identity. That is, modern conceptions of criticism espouse dialectical reasoning as the predominant image of thought. Difference thus "remains subordinated to identity, reduced to the negative, incarcerated within similitude and analogy."[2] Deleuze wants to diagnose, disrupt, and reconstitute the normative standing of the negative by transforming difference from a condition of lack into one of abundance. Like Jabès, Deleuze experiments with the idea that difference is not inherently nihilistic, that there is such a thing as difference in itself (rather than merely the quality of diversity), and that this difference is a generative force that creates relations.

In chapter 1 we saw how Hobbes's interest in a science of politics is entwined with his equally persistent commitment to distorted perspectives. Like the viewer of Holbein's *The Ambassadors*, Hobbes's citizen is defined by his or her capacity to produce a distorted account of the sovereign; that is, one of the powers of citizenship is to represent an image of sovereignty that might seem distorted from the perspective of everybody else. Similarly, Deleuze's attack on "the banality of the negative" wants to recuperate a conception of difference not circumscribed by an ideal of correct representations. By problematizing the truth-status of knowledge claims, Deleuze, like Hobbes, questions whether an account of political thinking committed to the pursuit of permanent resolutions is adequate to political inquiry and to political life more generally.

In the following I explain the role that Deleuze's philosophy of difference has in establishing a connection between thinking and political action. Not unlike Marx's attempt to overturn Hegel and derive a materialist political philosophy from the latter's idealism, Deleuze wants to overturn Plato in order to expose the materiality of thinking. In doing so, he pursues an "ethics of the problem" that tries to do away with the moral distinction of good and bad representations. Deleuze's poetics of political thinking turns to "paradox" as a source for thinking: Paradoxes, he argues, are not problems to be resolved. Rather, they illustrate elements of thinking that are the forgotten, nomadic fragments that predate thought. Thinking begins in the zone of indiscernability characteristic to paradox. This positive account of paradox—much indebted to an early modern mindset that underscores much of Deleuze's work—presumes a metaphysical pluralism that informs his more pronounced political objectives. In short, Deleuze's privileging of paradox as a source of thinking helps illuminate the contours of a democratic metaphysic characterized by the persistent simultaneity of coexisting dissimilars.

A Family Feud

ON TRIPLETS   In *Rabelais and His World*, Mikhail Bakhtin wonders why, of all the great European writers, Rabelais is the least appreciated and the least understood. To Bakhtin, the answer appears simple: We have lost the ability to laugh at Rabelais's works, because we no longer have the relationship to laughter that these works demand.[3] More important, modern readers have lost the ability to appreciate the grotesque (and its image of bodily excess) to such an extent that our responses to Rabelais are typically ones of embarrassment and disgust at the vulgarity of his images. In one of the more revealing passages, Bakhtin explains how contemporary attitudes to laughter are structured by a fundamental opposition between life and death. "Such an opposition," he continues, "is completely contrary to the system of grotesque imagery, in which death is not a negation of life seen as the great body of all the people but part of life as a whole—its indispensable component, the condition of its constant renewal and rejuvenation."[4] The grotesque presumes a circulating grammar of highs and lows: images of decay, filth, and the "bodily lower stratum" function as part and parcel of the generative motif that produce images of life, growth, and illumination. Death is not separate from life, it is the precondition for life's renewal; a dead body decays and fertilizes the soil, providing life's nourishment.

Consider a similar sentiment expressed by Rabelais's contemporary, Michel de Montaigne: "Death is the condition of your creation, it is part of you; you are fleeing from your own selves. This being of yours that you enjoy is equally divided between death and life. The first day of your birth leads you towards death as toward life."[5] Montaigne's "equally divided" self not only evokes an Augustinian notion of a split self—split, that is, by a Manichean struggle between the sacred and profane—but also describes natality as conditioned by the passing of time. The ultimate paradox of the last line—that the first day of one's birth is also the first step toward death—forces the reader to consider existence as a realm where life and death are complicit rather than separate.[6]

A substantive philosophical point ensues: the structure of grotesque imagery rejects the nihilism of negation. "In the private sphere of isolated individuals," Bakhtin concludes, "the images of the bodily lower stratum preserve the element of negation while losing almost entirely their positive regenerating force. Their link with life and with the cosmos is broken, they are narrowed down to naturalistic erotic images."[7] The isolationism of the private sphere nurtures the vulgarity that characterizes modern understandings of Rabelaisian humor. This reduces our understanding of the bodily lower stratum to something equivalent to mere pornography. On Bakhtin's account, however, negation ought always to preserve the simultaneous and paradoxical affirmation of a life force. To be sure, this does not guarantee that the relation between negation and affirmation is dialectical. The two forces are mutually dependent; in the absent nothingness of negation, one finds the life-giving potential of renewal and rejuvenation. The coextensiveness of these forces is a paradox that captured the imaginary of an early modern mindset.[8]

But what is it about paradox that is so appealing? Certainly, we must concede that the Renaissance attitude toward paradox is very different from our own. Consider W. V. O. Quine's exemplary discussion of paradoxes in philosophical argument:

> All these antinomies, and other related ones, can be inactivated by limiting the guilty principle of class existence in a very simple way. The principle is that for any membership condition you can formulate there is a class whose members are solely the things meeting the condition. We get Russell's antinomy and all the others of its series by taking the condition as nonmembership in self, or the like. Each time the trouble comes of taking a membership condition that itself talks in terms of membership and nonmembership. If we withhold our principle of class existence from cases where the membership condition mentions membership, Russell's antinomy and related ones are no longer forthcoming.[9]

Zeno's paradox, Russell's antinomy, the paradox of Empimenides—all of these are analyzed in terms of their logical structure, with an emphasis on their linguistic cogency. What this requires, according to Quine, is the "inactivation" of "the guilty principle" implied in the conceptual schemes that structure the paradox, so that logical mistakes such as categorial errors may be corrected. Paradox falls under the category of a moral mistake for Quine (why else make an appeal to guilt?)—a negative mark that with the right kind of work may be purged from one's thinking.

Renaissance writers, on the other hand, felt little guilt about paradox and spent much of their time "activating" its thought-provoking potential. Paradox fell into the category of the *ars rhetorica* and, as such, Rosalie Colie explains, was considered "an ancient form designed as *epideixis*, to show off the skill of an orator and to arouse the admiration of an audience, both at the outlandishness of the subject and the technical brilliance of the rhetorician."[10] There was much pleasure in paradox—perhaps as much pleasure as in the grotesque.[11] In order for it to produce its intended effects, paradox was never wholly divorced from logic but rather intertwined logic with received public opinion. "The subject of a rhetorical paradox," Colie explains, "is one officially disapproved in received opinion—and what is opinion, received or otherwise, but the dialectical opposite of 'truth'?"[12]

Thus the family feud. Philosophy (truth's domicile) and rhetoric (the domain of persuasion) have never been on good terms with one another, and if we can speak of a family resemblance between philosophy and rhetoric, then we might consider paradox the annoying cousin no one likes.[13] The fact of the matter is that paradox is both the black sheep of philosophy (to the extent that it revels in logical puzzles) and a starting point for rhetoric (to the extent that it lures an audience by surprise).

Stanley Fish's *Surprised by Sin* elegantly summarizes the contours of this family feud. In Milton's *Paradise Lost* Satan is the master rhetorician: "By first 'intangling' us in the folds of Satan's rhetoric, and then 'informing us better' in 'due season,' Milton forces us to acknowledge the personal relevance of the Arch-fiend's existence; and, in the process, he validates dramatically one of western man's most durable commonplaces, the equation of rhetorical appeal (representative of the world of appearances) with the weakness of the 'natural man,' that is, with the 'defects of our hearers.'"[14] "The defects of our hearers" is also the title of the first chapter of Fish's book.[15] The expression originates in Aristotle's *Rhetoric*, but Milton uses it to describe the power dynamics at work in any deliberative scenario. Indeed, book 2 of *Paradise Lost* may be read as an archetypal scene of republican debate where each of the devils represents a characterology of argumentative style.[16] Emphasizing this element, Fish's reading of Milton also highlights the extent to which the persuasiveness of rhetoric (i.e., the intangling) is at odds with critical analysis. In the Renaissance, he explains, the lure of rhetoric was met with not only resistance but also fear: "The deep distrust, even fear, of verbal manipulation in the seventeenth century is a recognition of the fact that there is no adequate defence against eloquence at the moment of impact."[17] This moment of impact, the moment of aesthetic experience, is also the instant when we realize that we have been "surprised by sin" by having been persuaded by Satan's eloquence. The deep distrust and fear of speech lies in the fact that, as fallen beings, we lack both the time and the cognitive ability to adequately reflect, critically evaluate, and subsequently deliberate upon potentially coercive utterances. What structures the rhetoric/philosophy feud is an Augustinian anxiety that our bodies—the receptors of aesthetic experience and source of humanity's lapse—will lead uncritically toward evil. Complementing this fear of rhetoric is a faith in self-reflection and, more precisely, a faith in dialectical reasoning as the diagnostic means by which we can correct defective thoughts.[18] *Paradise Lost* relies on this commonplace to the extent that Milton "draws upon the tradition of didacticism which finds its expression in a distrust of the affective and an insistence on the intellectual involvement of the listener pupil; in addition, he could rely on his readers to associate logic and the capacity for logical reasoning with the godly instinct in man and the passions, to which rhetoric appeals, with his carnal instincts."[19]

As an extension on Fish's treatment of rhetoric in the early modern period, Debora Shuger argues for a third element in the family feud: the sophist. She claims that in the Renaissance, rhetoric was as indebted to Hellenistic texts as it was to Roman ones. From these Hellenistic writings, Shuger derives the origins of "sacred rhetoric," concluding that "Hellenistic rhetoric does not support the division between rhetoric and philosophy as ontological antagonists."[20] Instead, sacred rhetoric distances itself from the playfulness of sophistry and imagines itself compatible with "serious philosophy." As Shuger makes abundantly clear, rhetoric is a necessary component for conversion and, as a consequence, could not be as easily banished to the dark side as Fish suggests: "The criticism of passionate rhetoric as sophistic flattery and play fails because it ignores the Renaissance's unplatonic view of the seriousness of rhetoric."[21]

Despite the Renaissance's "unplatonic views," Shuger points to the most Platonic of all structures at work in this feud. Though she rightly considers the sophist as an overlooked member of the family, by introducing this third element she exemplifies the tripartite structure of Plato's aesthetics at the heart of his politics and metaphysics: the Model (philosopher), the copy (rhetorician), and the simulacra (sophist). This aesthetico-philosophic triplet is Deleuze's starting point for his "reversal" or "overturning of Platonism" that sources his own image of political thought: "Everything may be traced back to the Platonic problem of participation," he asserts. "Plato proposed various hypothetical schemes of participation: to participate was to be part; or to imitate; or even to receive something from a demon. . . .

Participation was understood, according to these schemes, either materially, or imitatively, or demonically."[22]

DELEUZE'S "REVERSAL OF PLATONISM" As an image of thought, as a conceptual artifact possessing apodictic postulates that determine the operation of thinking, Platonism has practical repercussions.[23] It is a mode of classification that orders thoughts. The governing activity in Platonism is to determine, through the predicative function of resemblance, which copies are good and which are "false pretenders." "As a consequence of searching in the direction of the simulacrum and of leaning over its abyss," Deleuze asserts, "Plato discovers, in the flash of an instance, that the simulacrum is not simply a false copy, but that it places in question the very notations of copy and model."[24]

The language of suddenness that appears in Deleuze's account of Platonic thinking implies a rejection of the tranquillity of dialectical reflection. Dialectics is a slow process; Socratic dialogues are testament to its terrapin pace. Ideas, on the other hand, emerge in the "flash of instant," amid the chaos of speed. Qualifiers like "suddenness" and "velocity" illuminate Deleuze's principal claim for thinking: if the simulacra is characterized by disorder—by demonic participation—then thinking *is* simulacra. For Plato to have discovered the simulacra "in the flash of an instant" suggests a moment when Plato was captured by thinking and was entertaining the simulacra as a viable image of thought. In associating the simulacra with sophistry, Plato acts in bad faith by creating limits to the forms of participation available to those who think.

There is a moral struggle waged at the level of thinking, and the critical effect of reversing Platonism is to uncover the normative dimensions of the aesthetico-philosophic triplet. By *normative* I am referring to the procedural conditions for evaluation that determine a good and bad copy. Consider, in this regard, the process of resemblance. Deleuze tells us that in the Model-copy-simulacra relation, "the copy truly resembles something only to the degree that it resembles the Idea of that thing."[25] Resemblance, then, is not merely an associative principle but an organizational one as well. That which most closely relates to the Model does so on the principle of resemblance, making it a good copy. The procedurally normative dimension to Platonism lies in selecting good copies from bad ones: "For if copies or icons are good images, it is because they are endowed with resemblance. But resemblance should not be understood as an external relation. It goes less from one thing to another than from one thing to an Idea, since it is the Idea which comprehends the relations and proportions, constitutive of the internal essence."[26] As an associational power, resemblance is also an evaluative standard.

Deleuze's insights into Platonic formalism are not limited to Plato's hierarchical aesthetics, metaphysics, and politics. What differentiates Deleuze from other critics of Plato is his further insight that the competition for priority status among representations is not between Model and copy but between the Model/copy couplet and simulacra: "The function of the notion of the model is not to oppose the world of images in its entirety," Deleuze explains, "but to select the good images, the icons which resemble from within, and eliminate the bad images or simulacra."[27] The aesthetico-philosophic triplet makes the Model/copy couplet sovereign because the copy gives us mediated access to the Model through symbolic—rather than diabolic—representation.[28] It is thus "not a question of dividing a determinate genus into definite species, but of dividing a confused species into pure lines of descent, or of selecting a pure line from material which is not.... The meaning and the goal of the method of division is selection among rivals, the testing of claimants."[29]

There are, in Plato, true and false claimants for representation, and subsequently true and false copies; the sophist "lays claim to everything without a right."[30] Because their mode of engagement is demonic, the sophists are not able to make legitimate claims to other participants; their speech has no grounds for legitimacy: "Such, according to Plato, is the 'sophist,' the buffoon, centaur or satyr who lays claims to everything, and who, in laying such claims to everything, is never grounded but contradicts everything, including himself."[31] Resemblance grounds legitimacy in Platonism, which, in turn, implies a commitment to the law of noncontradiction. One who contradicts both the order of resemblance and him- or herself is not able to make claims on behalf of him- or herself. That is, the possibility of making claims presumes an a priori relation to the Model, a prima facie acceptance of the moral hierarchy implied in that ordering, and the ability not to contradict one's self. Sophists cannot take part in this, because they are the "demonic participants" who "contradict everything" at the outset.[32]

This politically charged language of claims, claimants, rights, and participation is consistent throughout Deleuze's treatment of Platonism. Such language points at the normative dimension of aesthetic evaluation and illuminates the credentialing institution of Platonism in modern life more generally. Unlike Jacques Derrida's critique of logocentrism, however, Deleuze is not interested in eliminating Platonic formalism per se, nor is he committed to the aporetic limits of representation as such.[33] Rather, his project is one of "overturning" while retaining the original formal structure. To regard the aesthetico-philosophical triplet merely as a formal principle of classification would thus miss its material effects as an image of thought. The fact that Plato explains his aesthetics as well as he does in *The Republic* is no mere coincidence. Given the procedural requirements of the aesthetico-philosophic triplet that ground the selection of lineages, political consequences must follow:

> Justice alone is just, says Plato. As for those whom we call the just, they possess the quality of being just in second, third or fourth place ... or in simulacral fashion. That justice alone should be just is not a simple analytic proposition. It is the designation of the Idea as the ground which possesses in first place. The function of the ground is then to allow participation, to give in second place. Thus, that which participates in varying degrees is necessarily a claimant. The claimant calls for a ground; the claim must be grounded (or denounced as groundless).[34]

The political effectiveness of this description is in its misrepresentation of Plato. At no point in *The Republic* does Plato argue that the determination of justice is a question of appeals or claims. In fact, this is what he finds distasteful about democracies and the demos more generally. Deleuze, on the other hand, situates Plato's treatment of justice within a contestatory context of claims and appeals, leaving one to conclude not only that Deleuze's image of political thought is radically democratic (this is hardly a surprise) but also that the activity of thinking itself is equally insurrectionist in that it mirrors the "unquiet" of the demos.[35] The treatment of Plato's hierarchies, and the obvious flirtations with a modern language of sovereignty, further testify to Deleuze's desire to situate Plato in conversation with modern debates about the adequacy of deliberation for democratic practice. Given that the tautology "justice alone is just" is the standard against which claimants must compare themselves, then those who don't stand within this closed circle of justice are those who "are never grounded and contradict everything, even themselves."

The critical thrust of Deleuze's "reversal of Platonism" is to determine how standards of aesthetic evaluation source our normative and political commitments. Overturning Platonism means questioning the apodictic stature of evaluative standards: "To reverse Platonism," Deleuze concludes, "means to make the simulacra rise and to affirm their rights among icons and copies."[36] The affirmation of the rights of the simulacra means the affirmation of all the qualities of simulacra: the right to contradict, the right to incoherence, the right to make false claims—namely, the right to indulge in a demonic mode of thinking and participation. Not, that is, because these rights are proper to democratic politics per se but rather, because there is nothing that guarantees a prima facie priority of the icons and copies over the simulacra.

Deleuze does not give up on the idea that political thinking—to the extent that it is a mode of thinking that posits the possibility of people and things relating—involves a substantive metaphysical register. The organizational structure of the aesthetico-philosophical triplet implies a hierarchical transcendentalism that dictates the manner in which individuals relate. The mode of attending to the metaphysical problem of relationality—that is, the forces that attract and distance bodies in space and time—is thus of primary political significance. With this in mind, Deleuze concludes that "with Plato, a philosophical decision of the utmost importance was taken: that of subordinating difference to the supposedly initial powers of the Same and the Similar, that of declaring difference unthinkable in itself and sending it, along with the simulacra, back to the bottomless ocean."[37] He expands on what it might mean to "think difference in itself" in his treatment of the univocity of Being.

A Nothing Drunk with Fullness

THINKING THE UNTHINKABLE   Before the introduction and acceptance of the number zero in Europe, there was immense computational confusion, because there was no signifier for absence. Brian Rotman explains,

> An iconic, mimetic approach to the writing of this absence might be the use of an empty space to signify it; so that for instance
>
> 11, 1 1, 1 1, 1 1
>
> would notate eleven, one hundred and one, one thousand and one and ten thousand and one respectively.[38]

This practice, espoused for thousands of years by Babylonian mathematicians, could not be used by early modern merchants to balance their ledgers because of its evident imprecision, especially given the differences in handwriting and the lack of mechanical devices guaranteeing a standard measurement between the numbers.

The mathematician Robert Kaplan signals double-entry bookkeeping as an important historical moment for the number zero. For Kaplan, the adoption of zero to balance a ledger marks the legitimation of the Arabic numerical system in the Western world. Profits and losses were doubly entered, thereby "creating a second, nominal account of profits and losses to which the profits, say, from the first account were transferred, this transfer listed therefore as a trading account debit. From the imbalance of this second account you could instantly see how your business was doing."[39] If the difference between one's credits and one's debts is zero, Kaplan explains, one's books were balanced, making them "good" books. This affirmative view of the number zero, and the balanced ledger it allows, helped legitimate the pursuit of profit through interest; the plus and minus column of the ledger illustrates the lender's risk that then justifies the lender's compensation for providing a loan.[40]

The "problem of nothing," exemplified in the debates surrounding the number zero, is not exclusive to merchant traders. In fact, these debates are the culmination of centuries-long theological disputes. Michael Camille's description of Remiet, a late-fourteenth-century illuminator, is exemplary in this regard. We know of Remiet's name and personage not because of something he did, but because of something he didn't do. In an otherwise fully illuminated manuscript by Guillaume de Deguileville (titled *Pèlerinages*), there is an instruction in the margins that asks Remiet "to make nothing here." Camille raises the point that medieval manuscripts were completely covered with decorations and illuminations, because of a *fear* of nothing. There was anxiety regarding vacant spaces in the period—an anxiety "which is evidenced in everything from scholastic discussions of nature's abhorrence of the vacuum to decoration of house wares."[41] To be told to "make nothing here" could not have sounded good to Remiet and, indeed, might have provoked great fear. "Within the framework of reading," Camille explains, "every part of the page, from running-title at the top to *bas de page* in the bottom margin, filled a void to excess in the form of vines, curling scrolls and snapping dragons, completing the book's appearance as a luxury object. In medieval discourse a complete thing automatically ranked above an incomplete one. 'Nothing' could even be lavishly completed and painted in gold and colors."[42] The idea that a blank page represents some form of incompletion is a familiar sentiment to modern readers, especially to those who have experienced the anxiety of writer's block. But the extended notion that blankness per se, anywhere on a sheet of paper, or in a book, has dire theological implications is, for us moderns, difficult to grasp. And yet, for someone like Remiet, this sentiment is absolutely valid. In fact, Remiet's entire life and work were dedicated to the seemingly impossible task of "filling a void to excess."

Remiet's dilemma and the advent of the cipher zero into merchant European ledgers are particular instances of a larger theological concern with the question of nothingness. Augustine's assertion, in his *Confessions*, that absence is tantamount to evil was the starting point for many disputes regarding God's role before creation.[43] Is *creatio ex nihilo* even conceivable given the existence of a benevolent god? Many medieval theologians grappled with the paradoxical relationship between void and excess; among the most illuminating and influential of these discussions were the arguments proffered by the Franciscan monk John Duns Scotus (A.K.A. Doctor Subtilis, 1266[?]–1308).

For Duns Scotus, the idea of negation compels the metaphysical question of relation: How does multiplicity relate to Being? What force is it that relates beings to Being? Duns Scotus's answer is that a "univocity of Being" enables an association between disparate entities, but not on the basis of analogy. Rather, Being relates to beings through predication: "God is thought of not only in some concept analogous to that of the creature, that is, one entirely different from what is predicated of a creature, but also in some concept univocal to himself and to a creature. And lest there be any contention about the word 'univocation,' I call that concept univocal that has sufficient unity in itself that to affirm and deny it of the same subject suffices as a contradiction."[44] In contrast to the Judeo-Christian claim that we are all made in God's image, Duns Scotus argues that our similarity to God exists because all beings possess univocity; God, then, is not merely analogous to other beings but is univocal both to himself and to others. The first sentence of the passage teaches us that God is univocal of all creatures (i.e., present to all creatures) and "entirely different from what is predicated of a creature." By retaining the principle of absolute difference between Being and beings, Duns Scotus makes difference in itself the first quality of Being. Associations, then, cannot be premised on analogy, since Duns Scotus is not positing a resemblance between God and beings. Rather, he is positing a univocity of Being that asserts the radical difference between particulars while relating them to one another.

Alain Badiou's book *Deleuze: La clameur de l'Etre* is helpful in clarifying some of this metaphysical murkiness. As Badiou points out, the principle of univocity cannot be understood numerically, in terms of the primacy of one-ness:

> The (principle of) univocity does not signify first and foremost that being is numerically one, which would make for an empty assertion. The One does not belong here to the order of counting or of identity, and the intellect has already given up if it imagines that there is a self-identical Being. . . . Univocity is neither in the order of a tautology (the One is One). It is, rather, fully compatible with the existence of multiple forms of Being.[45]

Badiou's explanation is insightful. One must not presume that univocity indicates singularity and, more important, one must not presume that univocity requires us to think Being as identity. Potentiality—the predicative principle of Being—presupposes that Being exists not only as a singularity but also as a multiplicity. If Being is univocal, then, it is said to exist in all the multiple forms of being—not because these forms are similarly different, but because they are differentiable. The principle of the univocity of Being in Duns Scotus—as Badiou's explanation evinces—is an associational principle grounded in the idea that difference in itself is a force or intensity rather than a quality.

Keith Ansell Pearson is surely right to claim that "the question of Being as univocal cannot be avoided in any appreciation of, or encounter with, Deleuze."[46] One only needs to read Deleuze's own assertion, at the outset of *Difference and Repetition*, that "there has only ever been one ontological proposition: Being is univocal. There has only ever been one ontology, that of Duns Scotus" to get a clear indication of his indebtedness to this subtle principle.[47] Deleuze explains his indebtedness to Duns Scotus further, in *The Logic of Sense*:

> The univocity of Being does not mean that there is one and the same Being; on the contrary, beings are multiple and different, they are always produced by a disjunctive synthesis, and they themselves are disjointed and divergent, *member disjuncta*. The univocity of Being signifies that Being is Voice that it is said, and that it is said in one and the same "sense" of everything about which it is said. That of which it is said is not all the same, but Being is the same for everything which it

is said. It occurs, therefore, as a unique event for everything that happens to the most diverse things . . . The univocity of Being merges with the positive use of the disjunctive synthesis which is the highest affirmation.[48]

The principle of univocity marks both an ontological turn in the conception of difference and a "minor event" in the history of philosophy. By weaving that historical thread from Duns Scotus, through Spinoza, to Nietzsche, Deleuze presents a counterhistory of metaphysics that illuminates the "banality of the negative." Importantly, this historical trajectory is also part and parcel of his overturning of Platonism—to the extent that Plato, in the flash of an instant, was the first to confuse difference with negation by denying simulacra their proper place among philosophical claimants.

The Banality of Dialectics

Deleuze's distaste for the law of noncontradiction is most strongly felt in his aversion to Hegelian dialectics, the most recent instantiation of the confusion of difference with negation. Consider this passage that Deleuze finds in Hegel's *The Science of Logic*:

> Difference as such is already *implicitly* contradiction. . . . Only when the manifold terms have been driven to the point of contradiction do they become active and lively towards one another, receiving in contradiction the negativity which is the indwelling pulsation of self-movement and spontaneous activity. . . . More precisely, when the difference of reality is taken into account, it develops from difference into opposition, and from this into contradiction, so that in the end, the sum total of all realities simply becomes absolute contradiction within itself.[49]

Contradiction avoids problems by orienting itself to resolutions. There are ethical consequences to this process: The function of dialectics is to "comprehend" what is oppositional. This relationship determines the movement of the finite toward the infinite so that the infinite is always represented as the "nothing that is," contrasted with the real as the "is that is nothing." In order for the infinite to be that toward which the finite is moving, it must be the nonbeing of the finite. This process, one Hegel scholar notes, guarantees Being its telos: "If one wants to consider the finite, one must not consider the finite, but rather the infinite; in order to grasp being, one must grasp thought, the Idea; there are no things, there is only *reason*; there is no exclusive determinacy, a 'this right here,' that excludes its opposite, but a rational exclusion, a 'this together with that'—i.e., the unity of 'sameness' and 'otherness,' of 'being' and 'non-being,' of finite and infinite in the infinite."[50] In contrast to Hegel, Deleuze pursues a nonteleological conception of difference. The force of Deleuze's criticism of Hegel is to suggest that, on the dialectician's rendering, difference can no longer posit problems, nor can the thinking of difference be regarded as the science of the problematic. Rather, in designating "difference as negation," the dialectician reduces difference to the search for solutions, making the impetus to resolution thinking's goal. "To think" thus means "to resolve problems," to determine that which no longer contradicts, and to expel that which prevents unity in thought.

In contrast, Deleuze distinguishes between thinking and thought: thinking refers to a "positing," it is propositional in nature, and its mood is subjunctive; thought aggregates knowledge, it is structured by apodictic norms, and its mood is imperative. This distinction between the subjunctive and the imperative moods is critical for Deleuze's ethical orientation. The activity of thinking sustains an "ethics of the problematic"—an orientation to others that is of the nature of the proposition—that disrupts the resoluteness of presuppositions. In so doing, Deleuze challenges those forms of immanent critique indebted to Hegelian dialectics because they are at once insufficiently immanent and insufficiently critical of their own assumptions.

Deleuze's image of political thought carries with it the following critical insights: The confusion of difference with negation privileges judgment as the mode for political thinking. One's thoughts about justice, the good, and the organization of society presuppose standards of evaluation that become so habitual as to count as common sense. That is, to think according to the judgment model means that common sense designates which judgments are good ones, without having its own goodness questioned. Analogy is the operation that governs this legitimation process: common sense acts as that which is representative of a general order of being. "The most general form of representation," then, "is thus found in the element of a common sense understood as an upright nature and a good will. The implicit presupposition of philosophy may be found in the idea of a common sense as *Cogitatio natura universalis*. On this basis, philosophy is able to begin."[51]

The status of presuppositions is a problem—it is *the* problem for thinking—to the extent that true beginnings cannot begin with presuppositions. "Where to begin in philosophy," Deleuze asserts, "has always—rightly—been regarded as a very delicate problem, for beginning means eliminating all presuppositions."[52] Philosophical postulates presume an "everybody knows that . . . ," or a "no one can deny that . . . ." Such appeals to our inherited intuitions make our thoughts both comprehensible and comprehensive:

> Postulates in philosophy are not propositions the acceptance of which the philosopher demands; but, on the contrary, propositional themes which remain implicit and are understood in a pre-philosophical manner. In this sense, conceptual philosophical thought has as its implicit presupposition a pre-philosophical and natural Image of thought, borrowed from the pure element of common sense. According to this image, thought has an affinity with the true; it formally possesses the true and materially wants the true. It is *in terms of* this image that everybody knows and is presumed to know what it means to think.[53]

The question of beginnings, the propositional postulates of philosophy, the moral character of good thought, and the relation between an image of thought and common sense presume that we are all thinking; or, at least, that we know what it means to think and that this "we know" predates the activity of thinking itself.

Through his analysis of philosophy's orientation to common sense, Deleuze indirectly challenges the critical purchase of contemporary political thinking: If the standards of evaluation for thinking are not critically engaged, and the implicit power dynamics are not adequately justified, can there be a philosophical enterprise critical of political practices? His answer is implicit in his analysis: "common sense" is a "dogmatic, orthodox or moral image [of thought],"[54] and to recognize this is a first step toward a postdialectical model of critique. Deleuze's project thus refuses the opposition between veracity and doxa, truth and opinion. Because opinion constitutes a sense that is common, thereby setting the conditions for philosophical thinking, then common sense is not simply a postulate of truth but is the doxa required for the production of truth: in short, opinion is the unrecognized ground of philosophical thinking and the task of critique is to disrupt the stasis of doxa within thought.[55]

Deleuze wants to situate the event of thinking prior to the existence of thought; prior, that is, to the normative question "What counts as good thought?" If this move is reminiscent of Duns Scotus's treatment of creation, it is not surprising. For Deleuze, thinking is *creatio*: "The conditions of a true critique and a true creation are the same," he states and continues, "the destruction of an image of thought which presupposes itself and the genesis of the act of thinking in thought itself."[56] Thinking, critique, and creation are intertwined and designate a disruptive event that forms the crux of Deleuze's own image of political thought. By designating thinking as an event that predates the familiar, Deleuze transforms Plato's static account of reflection into a force operating in the world—that is, a disjunctive force of pure potentiality.

It should not surprise us, then, that Deleuze attributes to paradox the generative force of creation. *Para-doxa*—literally that which is counter to the doxa of common sense—operates beyond the scope of contradiction: "The force of paradoxes is that they are not contradictory; they rather allow us to be present at the genesis of contradiction"; further, "the power of paradox therefore is not at all in following the other direction, but rather in showing that sense always takes on both senses at once, or follows two directions at the same time."[57] At the heart of paradox are the contrarieties and contradictions that compel thinking: "The sign or point of departure for that which forces thought is thus the coexistence of contraries, the coexistence of more and less in an unlimited qualitative becoming. Recognition, by contrast, measures and limits the quality by relating it to something, thereby interrupting the mad-becoming."[58] The demonic participation in thinking (i.e., the mad-becoming) is interrupted by the intrusion of the dialect. Deleuze's own poetics of political thinking wants to disrupt the model of recognition by interrupting the logic of substitution: to critique is to think, in the sense of engendering a new beginning, and this disjunctive engendering is antagonistic to the synthetic force of dialectics.

As an "avatar of the tortoise," Deleuze contrasts his model of thinking to the dialectical image of thought.[59] The event of thinking is political to the extent that thinking is critique. Thinking, then, is the generative force of the proposition that disrupts the dogma of presuppositions. In this regard, the activity of thinking is in and of itself a form of political action: Deleuze wants to undo the structural division of the *vita activa* and the *vita contemplativa* and make contemplation a form of political action — not necessarily because it is public (though there is always a public character to thinking) but because the designation of what counts as good thought — the standard for cognitive legitimacy — is a political move imbued with power.

There is, then, an ethical imperative in Deleuze. But rather than basing this imperative on either the aporias of language or a consensus model of deliberation, Deleuze looks to a quasi-mystical, nonlinguistic register: "What is the agent," he asks, "this force that ensures communication?" In this domain of dissemblance, he concludes, "there is no *amicability*, such as that between the similar and the Same or even that which unites opposites. . . . The dark precursor is sufficient to enable communication between difference as such, and to make the different communicate with difference: the dark precursor is not a friend."[60] This "dark precursor" is the nonlinguistic principle of association that sustains the possibility of interaction between absolutely different entities. It is, in short, the principle of disjunctive synthesis that relates differences with each other — on the basis not of what makes them similar, but of what makes them different.

Unlike many of his linguistic-turn contemporaries who situate language at the starting point of thought, Deleuze's rejection of "presuppositions" and his subsequent adoption of disjunctive synthesis imply a rejection of language as the ground of thinking. We saw how thinking, critique, and creation are interrelated in such a manner as to fracture the dogmatic image of thought. By inverting the predicative element in communication from resemblance to disjunction, Deleuze completes his overturning of Plato. The force that engenders thinking and critique is the force of potential found in the dynamic element of difference in itself.

To this insight Deleuze also adds a cautionary note: to confuse potentiality with possibility is, ultimately, to revert to "the banality of the negative." Potentiality does not have a place in actuality, as possibility does, but rather is that force that intervenes in the actual through the "mad becoming" of thinking. In confusing potentiality with possibility, one misses the critical force of thinking: when thinking fractures thought, one senses, "in the flash of an instant," a swarm of potential thought-emergences. "The discovery in any domain of a plurality of coexisting oppositions," he concludes, "is inseparable from a more profound discovery, that of difference, which denounces the negative and opposition itself as no more than appearances in relation to the problematic field of a positive multiplicity."[61]

This project of reversals concludes with the espousal of "the question" as the first principle of an ethics for thinking; for Deleuze, the irresolute structure of the question sources the diabolic potentialities of thinking. It is in this sense, then, that we must understand the thrust of Deleuze's critical and political intervention in the history of philosophy—an intervention that defines thinking as critical action and that grounds an ethics of the problem in a metaphysics of difference:

> Being is also non-being, but non-being is not the being of the negative; rather it is the being of the problematic, the being of problem and question. Difference is not the negative; on the contrary, non-being is Difference. . . . Once we confuse (non)-being with the negative, contradiction is inevitably carried into being; but contradiction is only the appearance or the epiphenomenon, the illusion projected by the problem, the shadow of a question which remains open and of a being which corresponds as such to that question (before it has been given a response).[62]

The rejection of contradiction as an adequate mode of critique is ethical: it implies further a refusal to treat difference as mere diversity, of reducing the question of difference to a qualitative property. This also implies a rejection of the model of judgment: "It is enough to replace the model of judgment with that of the proposition," he asserts.[63] Judgment, on Deleuze's rendering, requires common sense. In this respect, he is thoroughly Kantian. But common sense is a problem for thinking, because the intuitions that comprise common sense deny the critical force of the new. This is why nonbeing is both central to Deleuze's metaphysics and persistently at risk of being confused with negation. To replace the model of judgment with that of the problem means to overcome the impetus to evaluation when we think. In so doing, the possibility of engaging in demonic participation is available to us.

However, the distinction and replacement of judgment with "the problem" is a surprisingly curious and, indeed, problematic move. Despite his rejection of the judgment model, Deleuze's entire critical project relies on a particular dimension of judgment—one that recuperates the aesthetic value of thinking by making a virtue of thought-fragments, demonic participation, and the like; that is, by conceiving of the event of thinking as a form of political action. Consider, in this regard, his principal claim that there is a moment, before decisions about justice are made, that compels the configuration and ordering of the ground upon which such disputes occur. Though this subsequent ordering may by dictated by an a priori image of "good thought," and though Deleuze's poetics of political thinking may be directed toward the articulation of such images, this does not deny the value of judgment for thinking. Rather, it makes judgment a condition of an ethics of "the problem" that we also recognized in Hobbes: a commitment to *discrimen* as that form of judgment attuned to differences rather than similitudes.

In his treatment of Lewis Carroll in *The Logic of Sense*, Deleuze pronounces one final judgment: "Carroll, yes; Camus, no."[64] The affirmation of Carroll over Camus is Deleuze in his most moralizing tone: With this assertion, he provides us with two competing accounts of agonistic politics, both of which are rooted in a philosophy of difference. The latter, represented by Camus, is existential and stands in for the nihilism implicit in negative accounts of difference as absence. The former, exemplified by the loss of the proper name that is repeated throughout all of Alice's adventures, is an affirmation of a "nothing drunk with fullness" that rejects the nihilism of difference as negation. By privileging the simulacra as a source for an affirmative conception of difference, Deleuze wants to rethink a modern theory of sovereignty for democracy and provide us with his own political ideal: a nonhierarchical and egalitarian form of political organization: a nomadic distribution.

Deleuze's slippage from a rejection of moral dogmatism to a brusque rejection of judgment is troubling, though not surprising. For him, judgment cannot be separated from the one who judges—that is, from an authoritarian image of power carried within a modern conception of sovereignty. Like his contemporary and friend Michel Foucault, Gilles Deleuze elaborates a model of political thinking that tries to "cut off the head of the King."[65] In this regard, Deleuze's project is a thoroughly modern attempt at limiting the coercive entanglements of authoritarian rule by developing an ethos of thinking that appreciates the simultaneity of aesthetic and moral judgment.

Though Deleuze refuses to acknowledge a division between the aesthetic and the moral and though he rejects the possibility of a postmetaphysical politics, his poetic commitment to a language of rights in his own image of political thought does a lot to illustrate the extent to which political battles fought in the name of freedom and equality parallel internal and infrasensible battles waged at the level of ideas. For Deleuze, there is no division between the *vita activa* and the *vita contemplativa*, between the private and the public. As his attempt at deriving a historical heritage for difference in itself in *Difference and Repetition* and *The Logic of Sense* evinces, a history of ideas is a history of political contestation that at once parallels and uncovers the "confusion of difference with negation."[66]

3

The Beautiful and the Sublime in Rawls and Rancière

> Value is the quality a thing can never possess in privacy but acquires automatically the moment it appears in public.
> —HANNAH ARENDT

Discrimination and Value

"Everybody discriminates [*dijudicare*]," Cicero remarked. Everybody "distinguishes between right and wrong in matters of art and proportion by some silent sense without any knowledge of art and proportion."[1] What is this "silent sense" about which Cicero speaks? How, in other words, do humans generate value?

In the early 1970s in the United States, a series of groundbreaking studies analyzing the relationship between judgment and political thinking attempted to address these questions. If it is possible to single out one individual providing the most influential of these studies, then John Rawls is that person. Jürgen Habermas punctuates Rawls's stature, asserting that *A Theory of Justice* "marks a pivotal turning point in the most recent history of practical philosophy."[2] Indeed, before the publication of *A Theory of Justice* liberalism seemed mired, in varying degrees, in utilitarianism. Rawls introduced Immanuel Kant—or at least a neo-Kantian moral outlook—to the liberal debate, dramatically altering the face of liberalism.

In the fall of 1970, as *A Theory of Justice* was going to press, another notable and influential political theorist, Hannah Arendt, delivered her lectures on Kant's *Critique of Judgment* at the New School for Social Research. In these lectures, Arendt argues that Kant's treatise on aesthetics contains the vestiges of a model for political thinking that looks to judging as a way of "thinking in company with others."[3]

Though not similar, both projects attest to the possibility of deriving principles of political thinking from a philosopher who never wrote a treatise in political philosophy. These works further attest to the necessity of inventing a new mode of public thinking in the midst of a political culture characterized by social and political upheaval. These were turbulent times indeed—some say times of crisis. Along with a war few dare justify even today, the looming threat of nuclear catastrophe and the struggles over racial segregation were further reminders of the need to fabricate a novel form of public reason. "A crisis," Arendt declares in an essay of the same period, "forces us back to the questions themselves and requires from us either new or old answers, but in any case direct judgments."[4] From both the tone and subsequent influence of Arendt's and Rawls's works, it is hard to overlook the fact that America, dismayed by repeated testimony of political misjudgments, was ripe for a new orientation in political thinking. The reception of this new orientation helped spark one of the most lively debates in political theory in recent years: the liberal/poststructural debate. I address certain features of this debate by attending to some selected writings of John Rawls and Jacques Rancière. Specifically, my aim in these pages is to provide an account of the aesthetic preconditions of contemporary political argument and to explore the role of value as a mobilizing concept in Rawls's and Rancière's respective images of political thought.[5]

Liberalism and Aesthetic Value

THE DISCOURSE OF VALUE   For many political thinkers today, moral reasoning is the most reliable means to publicly justify our value preferences. The image of political thought that identifies a procedural apparatus to help us schematize a hierarchy of values is, perhaps, the most recognizable approach to political thinking. Yet the rise of a modern concept of value in the eighteenth century is not divorced so easily from its aesthetic heritage. As such Enlightenment luminaries as David Hume and Adam Smith evince, "value" is a cluster concept that conjures up reflections into the nature of the beautiful, the sublime, political economy, and social and political life.[6]

Unlike these other thinkers, Immanuel Kant's contribution to eighteenth-century aesthetics is unique in its attempt at wresting beauty from interest. Paralleling his arguments about moral reasoning in the second critique (specifically, the role of the will that wills an action as universalizable), Kant's *Critique of Judgment* treats beauty as a thing-in-itself, devoid of any subjective interest other than the interest in beauty alone. Judgment and willing are two unmistakably different activities according to Kant, and by distinguishing reflective (or contemplative) judgment from determinative judgment, Kant emphasizes that difference.[7] Determinative judgment "lays down the law," if you will, and is that legislative mode of thinking characteristic of practical reason. Reflective judgment differs because it does not legislate; we *affirm* rather than declare an object beautiful and we *presume* that everyone understands such an affirmation. Consider the following passage:

> Both the agreeable and the good refer to our power of desire and hence carry a liking with them, the agreeable a liking that is conditioned pathologically by stimuli, the good a pure practical liking that is determined not just by the presentation of the object but also by the presentation of the subject's connection with the existence of the object, i.e., what we like is not just the object but its existence as well. A judgment of taste, on the other hand, is merely *contemplative*, i.e., it is a judgment

that is indifferent to the existence of the object: it [considers] the character of the object only by holding it up to our feeling of pleasure and displeasure. Nor is this contemplation, as such, directed to concepts, for a judgment of taste is not a cognitive judgment (whether theoretical or practical) and hence is neither *based* on concepts, nor directed to them as purposes.[8]

Three terms consolidate Kant's schemata: the agreeable, the good, and the beautiful. The agreeable gives us pleasure and is "pathologically" linked to sense stimuli; it is, in short, the domain of desire. We have a subjective interest in the agreeable because agreeable objects please us. The good is similarly subjective but unlike the agreeable (an effortless and passive pleasure), the good is a product of our will. We have a subjective interest in the good because, according to the categorical imperative, it is contradictory to reason and detrimental to freedom not to (Kant also describes the good as that which we "esteem" or "endorse").[9] Both the good and the agreeable require subjective interest: the former is expressed as will and the latter in terms of pleasure. This is what Kant means when he says that we have a practical interest in "the subject's connection with the existence of the object."

The beautiful requires an entirely different mind-set. Just as we ought not to consider others in terms of their use-value (in that the function of other people is not that of satisfying our subjective interests), we cannot have a personal interest in an object when judging its beauty. A judgment of beauty, as counterintuitive as this may seem, is a judgment *devoid* of any and all interest—devoid, that is, of desire. "From this perspective," one scholar notes, "aesthetic objects are, like memories, dreams, and similar imaginative states, every bit as autonomous as Kant argues they are. They are autonomous, however, not because they never are influenced by an external reality or because they cannot compete with or substitute for reality. *They are autonomous, rather, because they cannot be exclusively assigned to either subjectivity or objectivity.*"[10]

Aesthetic objects are beautiful despite our desire for them; they defy subjective or objective categorization because beauty, like freedom, is not a quality. A judgment is aesthetic, then, because it appreciates beauty regardless of the descriptive qualities of the object in question. This, however, doesn't mean that we don't possess a subjective interest in art. Rather, it means that when we make an aesthetic judgment we do so *despite* our subjective interests, precisely because beauty—like any other mental state—exists independent of its representations. In short, "unclassifiability" refers to the autonomy of beautiful objects rather than autonomy being a classification, or quality, of them.[11]

Kant believes that we agree that beauty exists but we disagree about its examples. In making this claim he rejects the adoption of procedural norms to guide aesthetic evaluation: "If we judge objects merely in terms of concepts, then we lose all presentation of beauty. This is why there can be no rule by which someone could be compelled to acknowledge that something is beautiful. No one can use reason or principles to talk us into a judgment on whether some garment, house, or flower is beautiful."[12] Because no rules guide judgments of beauty, Kantian aesthetics requires that we judge objects in and of themselves, without recourse to either normativity or proceduralism. At the same time, when we appraise a beautiful object we assume our judgment is universally acceptable because it is disinterested: "And yet," Kant continues from the passage above, "if we then call the object beautiful, we believe we have a universal voice, and lay claim to the agreement of everyone, whereas any private sensation would decide solely for the observer himself and his liking."[13] Note that Kant does not say that we *possess* a universal voice, nor do we determine that everyone must agree; we merely "lay a claim" to the matter. This voicing of a belief and laying of a claim makes it so that value belongs to the public domain; aesthetic judgment for Kant and many of his Enlightenment contemporaries both presumes and produces a commitment to sociability. In contrast to the private realm—where utilitarian calculations are the modus operandi—the beautiful relies on a condition of publicity and universal assent, though not universal agreement.

Remarkably, Kant's argument makes taste independent of an officially sanctioned authority. The implication is that anyone who experiences a beautiful object has the capacity to critique it. The complete refusal, on his part, to determine standards of taste goes part and parcel with Kant's belief that an aesthetic object is valuable despite our liking it. By attributing to aesthetic objects such an autonomous status, Kant invents a practice of aesthetic criticism—not, to be sure, because he is founding rules for appraisal but because judgment is authoritative in and of itself, without having to rely on either normativity or the identity of the person pronouncing the judgment.

I suggested that Kant's treatment of the beautiful parallels his treatment of the categorical imperative in the second critique. To clarify this claim, I want to return to the question of value and its relation to eighteenth-century utilitarianism. The project of the *Critique of Practical Reason* is to dislodge moral reasoning from the constraints of utilitarianism. Kant does not address the question of the good but rather takes up that of the right so as to ascertain the apodictic certainty of the categorical imperative. The right differs from the good; we will the right for its own sake, and this willing determines our freedom. Analogously, treating the beautiful as a thing in itself is, for Kant, the aesthetic equivalent to conceptualizing the right as an *a priori*. The crucial difference, however, is that Kant does not legislate rules for the beautiful because, as he argues, that would presume an interest in apodictic norms denying aesthetic evaluation its autonomy. In short, the application of rules to the determination of beauty would be coercive by definition.

By wresting beauty from interest, Kant distances himself from a utilitarian notion of value rooted in individual desire. Though beauty appeals to the senses—in that it requires sense perception—its determination is independent of private sensation. For Kant, the kind of "in my opinion" justification for judgments of taste often invoked in our day and age is nonsensical at best. Though an individual may experience a beautiful object in private, and though such an experience may be intensely personal, our endorsement implies a commitment to sociability—a commitment, that is, to imagining oneself in company with others. If we can speak of an aesthetic interest in Kantian terms, then it can only be—to invoke Arendt one more time—an *inter-est*, a principle of sociability where a judgment of beauty invites an other's response.¹⁴ Though not intended as a social project, this principle of publicity offers the possibility of sympathetic identification, even when one is alone.

Kant's view of sympathy grants access to his understanding of common sense—a crucial element of his aesthetics. If, as Frances Ferguson notes, the project of the *Analytic of the Beautiful* is "the project of analyzing one's pleasure in an object that has no necessary relation to a previously existing object of exchange or use,"¹⁵ then the function of common sense is to generate a disinterested interest in intersubjective experience; that is, because the beautiful occasions sympathy, it also occasions a *sensus communis* independent of normative preconditions.¹⁶ Kant offers us the following explanation:

> we must take *sensus communis* to mean the idea of a sense shared [by all of us], i.e., a power to judge that in reflecting takes account (a priori), in our thought, of everyone else's way of presenting [something], in order, as it were, to compare our own judgment with human reason in general and thus escape the illusion that arises from the ease of mistaking subjective and private conditions for objective ones, an illusion that would have a prejudicial influence on the judgment.¹⁷

Comparison—that intellectual activity that allows us to imagine ourselves as part of a series of others—is the cornerstone of reflective judgment, which, in its turn, is synonymous with both publicity and "enlightenment."¹⁸ By comparing our judgment with the enlarged fund of knowledge that is human reason, we "escape the illusion" of prejudice. Comparison also requires justification, or the ability to account for our judgments. Through accountability, Kant submits, we are able to distinguish our judgments from mere opinions or likings, thus making them truly autonomous. Accountability frees us from our "self-incurred tutelage,"¹⁹ and argumentation—the sine qua non of justification—is the means by which such a freedom is attained.

Ultimately, Kant's *Critique of Judgment* is not simply an inquiry into the nature of the beautiful. Coupled with his myriad of statements regarding the hows and whys of evaluation throughout his oeuvre (including his moral writings), Kant's discussions in the third critique suggest that the kind of differentiation between aesthetic and moral reasoning found in many neo-Kantian writings today is problematic at best. The human capacity to judge is not merely a faculty—a property of the mind—it is also a condition of political freedom grounded in aesthetic experience. The idea of an a priori freedom pursued and defended in the *Critique of Practical Reason* returns as a sensation of autonomy experienced through encounters with the beautiful in the *Critique of Judgment*.

Though not explicit, such a symbiotic relationship between aesthetic and moral reasoning also pervades John Rawls's theory of justice and his subsequent discussions of the nature of political liberalism. When we adopt a reading strategy that privileges Rawls's manner of writing over the content of his arguments,[20] we encounter two central aesthetic features crucial to the cogency of Rawls's political liberalism: the first is an account of representation rooted in mimesis and the second is a narratological description of public reason, the cornerstone of a successful political order. Representability, mimesis, and narrativity all work within Rawls's schemata to produce an image of political thought rooted in an aesthetics of the beautiful.

A RAWLSIAN AESTHETIC   In his landmark 1967 essay "Art and Objecthood," the art critic Michael Fried emphasizes the importance of shape to modernist art. Shape, Fried notes, defines modernist painting so that the standard for success or failure of a painting rests on "whether the paintings or objects in question are experienced as paintings or as objects, and what decides their identity as *painting* is their confronting of the demand that they hold as shapes. Otherwise," Fried concludes, "they are experienced as nothing more than objects."[21] Contemporary political thought, like modernist art, is similarly committed to shape as a criterion for the success or failure of a legitimate political idea. Consider, for instance, John Rawls's language of a "framework of thought"[22] used to describe the procedural elements of his theory of justice. More so than any other political thinker, Rawls insists on the importance of arranging one's ideas so as to create a just resemblance between one's preferences and the fund of public intuitions informing justice.

After the initial backlash from the publication of *A Theory of Jus-*

tice (1971), Rawls consumed a considerable amount of ink adjusting, modifying, reshaping, and consolidating his unique account of political liberalism and public reason. In this regard, one of the most startling concessions he makes to his critics is to count disagreement as a condition of justice, despite his insistence that political discussions ought to have reasonable agreement as an objective: "It is unreasonable," he asserts, "not to recognize the likelihood—indeed the practical certainty—of irreconcilable reasonable disagreements on matters of the first significance."[23] In part, this recognition of disagreement derives from his description of pluralist societies as possessing "reasonable comprehensive doctrines" that, in their own manner, dictate conditions for the good life. Indeed, Rawls characterizes the difference between *A Theory of Justice* and *Political Liberalism* in precisely these terms: In *A Theory of Justice*, justice as fairness is a comprehensive liberal doctrine, whereas *Political Liberalism* asks "how is it possible for those affirming a comprehensive doctrine, religious or nonreligious, and in particular doctrines based on religious authority, such as the Church or the Bible, also to hold a reasonable political conception of justice that supports a constitutional democratic society?"[24] Whereas *A Theory of Justice* provides us with a procedure for moral justification, *Political Liberalism* asks what conditions need exist for such a procedural mechanism to work at all. This suggests that one of the key differences between Rawls's early and later writings is the appearance of the word *political* in his title.[25]

With this increased appreciation of pluralism, Rawls recognizes that the exposition of "a theory of justice" is insufficient for political life; one must also make the theory attractive by satisfying certain "burdens of reason" that include the condition of disagreement. Rawls makes a further point: Despite disagreement, individuals are born into a particular political culture that contains a variety of mutually recognized principles and ideals. In the case of democratic political cultures, freedom and the belief that well-organized institutions can guarantee freedom are among these shared principles. The fact that despite the plurality of comprehensive doctrines we are still able to agree on this as an ideal attests not only to the necessity, but also to the facticity, of an overlapping consensus.

The liberal citizen thus resides at the intersection of a political paradox: she is at once committed to her own conception of the good and to the stability of the political order within which she lives. That is, she is committed to the ideal of difference implicit in pluralism (the source of substantive disagreement), while relishing political harmony. To reconcile this paradox, Rawls asks the reasonable citizen to accept deliberation as the privileged mode of political action, specifying three essential elements therein: (1) an idea of public reason; (2) a framework of constitutionally founded democratic institutions that specify the setting for deliberative legislative bodies; and (3) the knowledge and desire on the part of the citizen to follow public reason.[26]

"As reasonable and rational, and knowing that they affirm a diversity of reasonable religious and philosophical doctrines," Rawls writes, "[citizens] should be ready to explain the basis of their actions to one another in terms each could reasonably expect others might endorse as consistent with their freedom and equality."[27] The valid terms for explanation are those specified by public reason, an ideal public vocabulary guaranteeing understanding among participants. To be sure, a liberal lexicon is not subject to a Kripkean primal baptism, but its status as the guarantor of understanding is.[28] "Each conception," Rawls further elucidates, "should express principles, standards, and ideals, along with guidelines of inquiry, such that the values specified by it can be suitably ordered or otherwise united so that those values alone give a reasonable answer to all, or nearly to all, questions involving constitutional essentials and matters of basic justice."[29] In short, public reason requires completeness as a condition for participation, including an outline of what it means to think politically. If this is not satisfied, then "it is not an adequate framework of thought in the light of which the discussion of fundamental political questions can be carried out."[30]

Like Kant's sensus communis, Rawls's public reason is premised on the idea of accountability. In order for individuals to be successful citizens, they must be able to give reasons for their beliefs and actions. That is, when matters of deliberation regarding constitutional essentials are at stake—synonymous, for Rawls, with politics as such—one must be ready to explain one's self in a manner that is understandable to others. Rawls understands public reason, and the overlapping consensus that he derives from it, as a horizon of reasonable interpretative arguments accessible because of shared intuitions: "We are required first to work out the basic ideas of a complete political conception and from there to elaborate its principles and ideals, and to use the arguments they provide. Otherwise public reason allows arguments that are too immediate and fragmentary."[31] Thus, although the political culture might be "immediate and fragmentary" and fraught with disagreements, public reason cannot be. What is more, the possibility of the perpetuation of a political system through time (i.e., the condition of its success) rests on the public exposition of arguments constituting the totality of public reason.

The themes of "completion," "reflective judgment," and "temporal perpetuity," along with the conviction that an idea's shape guarantees access to political participation, betray a commitment to a tacit aesthetic dimension of Rawls's thinking that is made less taciturn when we consider certain poetic principles that pepper his writing. At its most basic level, we recognize that what makes public reason "public" is its grounding in a linguistic model of communication and judgment. Deliberation requires language, and justification necessitates the exposition of the points of an argument. These burdens of accountability thus constitute political argument as praxis. The noteworthy absence of rhetoric as a source of persuasion also suggests that justification—because it is characterized by the compelling force of epistemology—is not coercive.[32] But if the speech category of "the argument" no longer resides in the domain of the ars rhetorica—as it once had in the North Atlantic and Mediterranean pedagogic imaginary—then perhaps it is safer to speak of an art of narration constitutive of political argument more generally.[33]

Arguments have plots. Hannah Arendt once remarked that "who says what is . . . always tells a story, and in this story, the particular facts lose their contingency and acquire some humanly comprehensible meaning."[34] A successful argument is one that people can follow; it directs the listener through the exposition of a series of points. An argument is at once episodic and meaningful; its temporality relies on serial progression, which makes an argument reasonable or logical. To follow an argument—by which we mean to understand an argument—refers specifically to that capacity of organizing scattered events into a serial succession that looks like a compositional whole.[35] This, in short, is the narrative power of argument.[36]

The explanatory procedures of the epistemology of an argument— the standpoint upon which justification and accountability rely—do not replace the narratological properties of public reason but function in tandem and in tension with them. Testifying to the intractable problems of translating intellectual works, Jonathan Rée punctuates this sentiment, asserting that "the translator of modern philosophy is not spared any of the problems of 'voice,' obliquity, and transparency that confront the translator of modern novels."[37] Indeed, these dimensions of narrativity shape an argument, making it possible for people to follow along. But "following along" is not passive; we confront the fragile totality of a narrative with our own horizon of expectations, producing tensions that may or may not be resolvable. The art of narrative that characterizes public reason at once assists and complicates our understanding of consensus: the confrontation of horizons that Ricoeur discusses throughout his writings on narrative suggest that the kind of dialogic encounter Rawls examines in deliberative exchange is more complicated than the procedural model allows. The hermeneutic fusion of horizons implies an ability to make an other's narrative one's own. But this compositional competence (which Ricoeur calls "refiguration") problematizes—if not limits altogether—the kind of substitutive operation that Rawls's commitment to mimetic representation relies upon.[38]

The aesthetic features of Rawls's account of public reason are not limited to their narratological dimensions. There is an ethics to his poetics rooted in a faith that anything is, in principle, representable. Representability—and mimesis as the shape that representation should take—grounds his appeal to justice as fairness and its commitment to creating a political system where inequalities are to benefit the least advantaged. This second of his two principles of justice implies that a fair political system can be devised and that the kinds of blindnesses associated with a utilitarian schema (that generates losers) are, indeed, avoidable if we accept the principle of the inexhaustibility of representation. This is what makes Rawls's schema uniquely universalist—not, that is, because it is meant to be imposed on everyone, but because it can be extended to everyone. Rawls's universalism is, as Drucilla Cornell rightly states, a universalism of scope.[39]

This universalism of scope finds its heritage in Kant's third critique. Paralleling Kant's account of the beautiful and the disinterested interest in an object of beauty, Rawls avoids at all costs the reduction of meaningful political interaction to a zero-sum game of competing interests. When one comprehensive doctrine's orientation is no longer neutral with respect to justice—so that what is at stake are competing conceptions of the good—then there can be no fairness. Thus Rawls's commitment to public reason as a principle of representation is ultimately a commitment to imagining democratic equality as an arithmetic sum $(n + 1)$; the inexhaustibility of representation means that anyone can be added to the list of participants in deliberation about matters of justice.

Rawls's investment in representation as such extends to granting citizens an innate capacity to mimetically represent public reason to themselves. Consider, in this regard, his treatment of the exemplarity of the Supreme Court as a credentialing institution: "The court's role as exemplar of public reason," he explains, "has a third aspect: to give public reason vividness and vitality in the public forum; this it does by its authoritative judgments on fundamental political questions. The court fulfills this role when it clearly and effectively interprets the constitution in a reasonable way; and when it fails to do this, as ours often has, it stands at the center of political controversy the terms of settlement of which are public values."[40] *Exemplarity* is an interesting term to use, as it inadvertently invokes an element of humanist rhetoric: imitation. By noting the exemplarity of the Supreme Court, citizens are asked to imitate not simply the court's judgments, but also its mode of reasoning. "Exemplarity" also possesses affective resonances that include such sentiments as sympathy, attachment, and awe—responses that are somatic as much as they are cognitive. Finally, there is a heroic aspect to exemplarity that recalls the epic poetry of the Greeks and Romans: Rawls's proceduralism and its juridical heritage are the heroes of the story that public reason tells of itself; they stand in as a kind of Odysseus or Aeneas for the modern woes of multicultural societies.

The effect of the court's exemplarity, like Nussbaum's account of the usefulness of the novel, is pedagogical: Supreme Court decisions engender a public spectacle that provides citizens with an ideal image of public reason in action. Moreover, the sentimental education embodied through the Supreme Court's exemplarity instructs citizens on the importance of neutrality when making political decisions. As long as one endorses the level of disinterestedness required for public deliberation, then any individual or group can add themselves freely to the list of participants.

From this perspective, Rawls's project of political liberalism starts to look like an attempt at institutionalizing sympathy in political society by transforming this properly moral sentiment into a political project. To conceive of sympathy as a procedure, rather than an emotion, means that the "free rider" is no longer a political concern. As David Hume noted, we would not need justice if benevolence were guaranteed, because the function of justice is to restore the wrongs done by those who do not possess this virtue.[41] Rawls similarly recognizes the relationship between justice and the virtue of benevolence, but he takes it one step further. Because there are no guarantees that the benevolence arising from sympathy will be the dominating force in political life, we must create a system that ensures sympathy as an outcome; that is, justice requires a procedural apparatus of sympathy to override the waning of individual wills.

Rawls's preference for a free-standing view of justice also invokes the parameters of Kantian reflective judgment. The basic structure stands as the object of aesthetic evaluation that citizens must appreciate in and of itself, without recourse to a subjective interest. However, Rawls cannot eliminate desire wholeheartedly from his image of political thought: that is, he requires a conception of the agreeable to encourage reasonableness. The perpetuity of the basic structure requires that one's evaluative criteria shift from a disinterested interest to a liking; this, in its turn, produces the need for rules: Whereas for Kant, the fund of intuitions allowing others to understand an aesthetic judgment—his sensus communis—is indeterminate (because it is not rule-governed), for Rawls it is imperative to derive norms that clarify the useful intuitions from the useless ones, the reasonable from the unreasonable. There is, then, a subjective interest in the procedures of public reason; political stability is that interest.

At stake in public deliberation is something more than the value of the dispute; deliberation instructs how to be sociable and is a requirement for citizenship. "Public discussion becomes more than a contest for power and position," Rawls asserts. "This educates citizens to the use of public reason and its value of political justice by focusing their attention on basic constitutional matters."[42] Like Kant's commitment to the sociability of aesthetic judgment, so too with Rawls does public deliberation alert citizens to the presence of others. The ability to give an account—that is, the ability to narrate the validity of one's reasons by formally representing one's ideas so that they mirror the spectacle of public reason—is equivalent to political action in the Rawlsian schema. This is the essence of politics that lies at the heart of Rawls's "political liberalism." Without accountability, politics cannot exist. What remains is a series of disjunctive, comprehensive doctrines that threaten freedom.

Included in the idea of public reason are certain aesthetic features that operate at the infrasensible layer of judgment—a level of appraisal that requires somatic, as well as cognitive, responsiveness. The presence of aesthetic preconditions for public reason such as narrativity and mimesis points to a heretofore unexplored poetics in Rawls's political thinking. Looking to his manner of writing and the kinds of things his account of reason relies on, we learn that our cognitive capacities, as well as our epistemological acumen, are insufficient on their own when confronting and responding to an other's reasonable comprehensive doctrine. At the very least, we must appreciate and learn to *acknowledge* what a comprehensive doctrine looks and sounds like.[43] We might have to learn how to curb our enthusiasm when we disagree with the shape or noise of this new horizon of judgment. Indeed, the burden of justification—a key precondition of participation in deliberative exchange—is a weight we experience and feel obliged to satisfy. In order for it to work at all, deliberation also requires a catharsis through self-revelation: Rawls presumes a kind of piety in deliberation where citizens must speak truthfully and sincerely about themselves. Finally, accountability in deliberation presumes not only that individuals present justifications for their actions and beliefs, but also that their reasons be experienced as disinterested, just as Kant's interest in the beautiful is disinterested. All these aesthetic markers are present yet unacknowledged in Rawls's arguments about the nature of political argument.

In attempting to safeguard politics by divesting it of subjective interest, Rawls creates an image of political thought that parallels Kant's conception of the beautiful in the *Critique of Judgment*. The neutral domain of public reason guarantees the freestanding view of justice its autonomy in the same manner that the disinterest in an object of beauty guarantees a judgment of taste its autonomy. In both instances, the threat of coercion is eschewed by situating judgment in a world apart from the mundane world of individual desire (in the case of Kant, subjective interest; in Rawls's case, comprehensive doctrines).[44] Rawls's claim that justice as fairness is "political" and not "metaphysical"[45] thus starts to look like a corollary to Flaubert's and Baudelaire's claims announcing the birth of *l'art pour l'art* in the second half of the nineteenth century. These latter figures, as Pierre Bourdieu has shown, also saw themselves as fulfilling Kant's aesthetic project by creating a literary field autonomous from the concerns of the social.[46] Rawls's conception of justice as freestanding—indeed, his entire outline for a uniquely *political* liberalism—similarly announces a politics-for-politics'-sake account of justice that is best understood under the lens of his tacit aesthetic commitments. The autonomy of the political that Rawls ardently defends is ultimately a rejection of the kind of social-interest group politics so prevalent in the latter half of the twentieth century. This is why he tries to devise an account of multicultural pluralism that is not social (by which he means independent of particular desires).

With this in mind, those challenges to the Rawlsian project that question the epistemic viability of liberal neutrality overlook a more relevant issue:[47] namely, can we have a project of politics for politics' sake that isn't, as Alessandro Ferrara notes, peculiarly antipoliti-

84 CHAPTER 3

cal?[48] A more compelling challenge to Rawls's commitments would thus put pressure on his aesthetics of politics and, indeed, the status of autonomy in Rawls's image of political thought.

Democracy and Dissymmetry

THE REVOLUTIONARY SUBLIME "The revolution, which threw the government into the hands of the penners and adopters of this declaration," wrote Jeremy Bentham in his *Anarchical Fallacies*, was being justified after the fact, after the damage was done. "But by justifying it," he continued, "they invite it: in justifying past insurrection, they plant and cultivate propensity to perpetual insurrection in time future; they sow the seeds of anarchy broad-cast: in justifying the demolition of existing authorities, they undermine all future ones, their own consequently in the number."[49] For Bentham, the danger of even attempting to formulate a justification for such a horrific travesty against authority as the French Revolution was a performative contradiction that would condemn further generations, and *The Declaration of the Rights of Man and the Citizen* (1791) was an excess of words that, having been published and circulated throughout Europe, sowed a principle of illegitimacy in what was the fertile terrain of political authority. Bentham's own *Anarchical Fallacies* was a futile (on his view) though necessary effort to undo the irreparable damage done by this sublime excess of words; an attempt, that is, to restore words to their proper place and grant them their poetic dignity that the *Declaration* withholds.

Preceding Jeremy Bentham, Edmund Burke was one of the first to characterize the events of 1789 in terms of an aesthetics of the sublime. Though Burke's status as a political thinker has long been acknowledged by political scientists and political theorists alike, his equally significant status as an aesthetician is often overlooked.[50] Like his German contemporary, Immanuel Kant, Burke was an astute student of aesthetics, who in 1757 published *A Philosophical Enquiry into the Origin of our Ideas of the Sublime and Beautiful*.[51] In this treatise Burke offers an empirical account of the sublime that treats the object of sublime experience subjectively—that is, as an experience derived from the sensations of "horror" and "terror":

> The passion caused by the great and sublime in *nature*, when those causes operate most powerfully, is Astonishment; and astonishment is that state of the soul, in which all its motions are suspended, with some degree of horror. In this case, the mind is so entirely filled with its object, that it cannot entertain any other, nor by consequence, reason on that object which employs it. Hence arises the great power of the sublime, that far from being produced by them, it anticipates our reasonings, and hurries us on by an irresistible force. Astonishment, as I have said, is the effect of the sublime in its highest degree; the inferior effects are admiration, reverence and respect.[52]

The term "astonishment" is key both in this text and in his later writings on the French Revolution, as we shall soon see. Burke's use of it refers to a state of stupor preventing further development and progress. The sublime is an irrational state; we are "astonished" precisely because our minds can't grasp the "irresistible" and excessive force of the sublime object: the mind is literally overflowing with this thing— so much so that "it cannot entertain any other, nor by consequence reason on that object which employs it."[53] The "astonishment" in the soul is an experience of excess that produces a sensation of horror. Burke's pedagogical metaphor of the mind as vessel is empiricist to the extent that it relies on sense experience as a source of intellectual fulfillment. Aesthetics for Burke, as for many of his contemporaries, including Hume, Smith, Rousseau, and Kant, serves a pedagogical purpose that the category of the sublime negates. Unlike the kind of pleasure one derives from the beautiful, the capacity for which also indicates a certain cultivation of taste, the sublime interrupts further development: by filling the mind with astonishment and terror, a sublime experience interrupts development and cultivation; that is, it interrupts history.

Frances Ferguson explains how Burke's account of aesthetic experience relies on a dialectic of the beautiful and the sublime:

> The beautiful, for [Burke], registers human sensation as a susceptibility to all the experiences that draw an individual into society. The

sublime is, in his view, likewise sensationist. Yet sensation here operates to produce two radically different sorts of effects: inducing social cohesion, or a commitment to a society, in the beautiful and precisely the reverse, or a commitment to self or self-preservation, in the sublime. For while Burke presents the beautiful as the sociable, he depicts sublime sensation as asocial (or even anti-social).[54]

By interrupting the flow of history as an experience available for human sensation, the sublime returns us to an antisocial state of radical individuality—radical, that is, because it generates within us a sense of solitude distancing us from others. This distance makes self-preservation, rather than sociability, our principal drive. Indeed, the sublime is so radically individuating that it forces us to confront our own mortality: "No passion," Burke asserts, "so effectually robs the mind of all its powers of acting and reasoning as fear. For fear being an apprehension of pain or death, it operates in a manner that resembles actual pain. Whatever therefore is terrible, with regard to sight, is sublime too."[55] The sublime is antisocial, then, because it is dissociative: it disorients our minds to such a degree that we find ourselves in a state of indiscernability that not only disrupts our mental faculties (most notably our capacity to judge) but also interrupts society as an organic and historical force.

In *Reflections on the Revolution in France*, Burke invokes his aesthetic writings to describe Europe's political climate after 1789:

> It looks to me as if I were in a great crisis, not of the affairs of France alone, but of all Europe, perhaps of more than Europe. All circumstances taken together, the French revolution is the most astonishing that has hereto happened in the world. The most wonderful things are brought about in many instances by means the most absurd and ridiculous; in the most ridiculous modes; and apparently, by the most contemptible instruments. Every thing seems out of nature in this strange chaos of levity and ferocity, and of all sorts of crimes jumbled together with all sorts of follies. In viewing this monstrous tragicomic scene, the most opposite passions necessarily succeed, and sometimes mix with each other in the mind; and alternate contempt and indignation; alternate laughter and tears; alternate scorn and horror.[56]

With characteristic eloquence and biting wit Burke's description reads like a theatrical review in the daily papers. In his office as both political critic and dramaturge, he opines to the dramaturgical failure of the French Revolution as evinced by the genre in-mixing of which this play is complicit. Note also the return of the term *astonishing*, the key sensation associated with the sublime. There is a crisis in all of Europe (not just France), and this crisis could be as much a crisis of aesthetic representation as it is one of political representation. At the heart of this crisis, the critic locates instances of unnatural copulations: "levity and ferocity," "crimes and follies" that produce "laughter and tears." Indeed, what the French Revolution produces is a "monstrous tragicomic scene" that is not merely unpleasant to the stability of Europe's political order (as Burke will later argue) but is also a poetic failure. Nothing fits in this "strange chaos," and "everything seems out of nature."

Once encountered, the revolutionary sublime pollutes the mind to such a degree that one can no longer rely on it for discernment. Moreover, we can no longer rely on traditional categories like the tragic or the comic, or even natural responses like laughter and tears, scorn and horror. Because of the in-mixing characteristic of the revolution, these perverse copulations threaten politics and society more generally. People value the Revolutionary Society, they claim that democratic appeals to an ideal liberty are progressive and enlightened, but, in truth, judgments fail because one's discriminatory competence is damaged by the distorting effects of the sublime: "The fresh ruins of France, which shock our feelings wherever we can turn our eyes," Burke concludes, "are not the devastation of civil war; they are the sad but instructive monuments of *rash and ignorant counsel* in time of profound peace."[57]

The French Revolution is not only a sublime event, it also a historical lesson that produces a sense of horror and, ultimately, social dissolution. The need to restore this politics gone awry is apparent throughout Burke's *Reflections* and, indeed, throughout his later writings. For him, the Revolution is as much a political miscalculation as it is a bad play. Things were placed together that do not belong there, excesses resulted, and the ability to judge is lost. In short, all the things Burke fears about the French Revolution supply Jacques Rancière's poetics of political thinking.

AN AESTHETICS OF TORT   Like Burke, Rancière recognizes the value of sense experience to political life. The scene of the "modern revolution" (by which Rancière means the democratic revolutions of the seventeenth and eighteenth centuries) is populated by an *excess of words*—that is, by a series of speakers who "speak too much, who speak incorrectly, out of place and outside truth."[58] In this regard, and again like Burke, Rancière articulates the emergence of democratic politics in terms of sublime dissonance. But whereas Burke saw this as an antisocial threat that instills division, Rancière treats the sublime as the sine qua non of political action, precisely because of its divisive nature. "The revolutionary event," he asserts, "that which we must not dissolve in the supposed effect of its causes, is precisely the opening of a new political space, characterized by the excess of spoken words."[59] The excess of words brings about an anachronistic speech situation—a characteristic feature of those who are not recognized as having a place from which to speak and must speak out of turn. In the remaining pages of this chapter I discuss Rancière's theme of "the miscount" as it relates to his conception of democratic politics. Most notably, the "miscount" of democracy stands as a condition of unrepresentability constitutive of democratic equality. Democratic politics, in short, is a temporality that prevails if, and only if, there is a failure of representation. Ultimately, for Rancière, democracy occurs whenever there is a miscount and when "the part of those who have no part" voices a wrong.

The French word *tort*. meaning either "fault" or "wrong," is important for English-speaking jurists, as it connotes the juridical category of the law of torts. For Rancière to base his image of democratic thinking on the word *tort*[60] and for him to define equality as a divisive element in politics is particularly significant given the rise of tort law and social contract accounts of political society in the eighteenth century. The regulative principle of a social contract, in its most general sense, is to guarantee the equal distribution of rights and obligations within a democratic regime. Concomitantly, tort law "involves questions of how people should treat one another and the rules of proper behavior that society imposes on each citizen for avoiding improper harm to others, and for determining when compensation for harm is due."[61] Yet tort is not simply a juridical category; it is also a social calculus informing our idea of retributive value. As such, it always carries with it a differential quality: tort implies a loss of value or, more to the point, a division of a totality, as William Blackstone specifies in his *Commentaries on the Laws of England*: "Tort law," he explains, "is the *remedial* [part of law] whereby a method is pointed out to recover a man's private rights, or redress his private wrongs."[62] Social contract theory and the law of torts complement one another (both historically and theoretically) to such a degree that it is difficult to imagine an account of a social contract without an (implicit and simultaneous) articulation of torts—that is, without an account of the obligations and duties of citizens and the penalties incurred for not executing these.

Translating the French *mésentente* as "disagreement" is accurate but inadequate.[63] An *entente* is an understanding, and a *més-entente* implies at once a disagreement and a misunderstanding. As Rancière describes it, *mésentente* refers to "a determined kind of speech situation: one in which one of the interlocutors at once understands and does not understand what the other is saying." Mésentente, then, "is not the conflict between one who says white and another who says black. It is the conflict between one who says white and another who also says white but does not understand the same thing by it or does not understand that the other is saying the same thing in the name of whiteness."[64]

Mésentente is not simply a misunderstanding; it is first and foremost a contest over the constitutive features of the speech situation itself. That is, mésentente is not an argument about the meaning of names; rather, it questions whether the operation of naming is an adequate corollary to democratic politics. Though invested in an account of the efficacy of speech acts, Rancière's point of departure ought not to be considered as an attempt at determining an ideal of communication. Rather, his interest is in exploiting the moment when the poetic specificity of meanings are not yet determined; that is, when the point of contention is not what a word means, but what it means for a word to signify. In so doing, he provides his readers with an account of the political efficacy of dissonance and senselessness. That is, Rancière intervenes in the discussions of democratic deliberation by shifting the focus from a discussion of words as entities pregnant with signification (and therefore belonging to the order of mimetic representation) to a state before referentiality, when semantic designation has not yet taken place.

The stated objective of *Dis-agreement* is to inquire into "the set of reflective operations whereby 'political philosophy' tries to rid itself of politics, to suppress a scandal in thinking proper to the exercise of politics."[65] This theoretical scandal, he goes on to explain, is nothing other than the "rationality of disagreement" whose history is rooted in the Ancient Greek *blaberon*, whence we derive our English "blabber."[66] In Aristotle's *Nicomachean Ethics*, the *blabê* refers to a disproportion that compels balance:

> Justice is a kind of mean, but not in the same way as the other excellences, but because it relates to an intermediate amount, while injustice relates to the extremes. And justice is that in virtue of which the just man is said to be a doer, by choice, of that which is just, and one who will distribute either between himself and another or between two others not so as to give more of what is desirable to himself and less to his neighbor (and conversely with what is harmful), but so as to give what is equal in accordance with proportion; and similarly in distributing between two other persons. Injustice on the other hand is similarly related to the unjust, which is excess and defect, contrary to proportion, of the useful or hurtful.[67]

Aristotle famously defines equality as proportion; injustice refers to an excess that produces harm. The blaberon, according to Rancière, becomes relevant for Aristotelian ethics when a wrong, resulting from an excessive imbalance, is voiced. For him, there is a history of the blaberon that coincides with a history of democratic politics. The blaberon illustrates the principle of illegitimacy proper to the concept of equality that opens a space for the voicing of an injustice. Democratic equality on this rendering is, by definition, disorderly, since the blaberon refers to an illegitimate arrangement.

Rancière's appeal to tort, implicit in his historical account of the blaberon, connotes a constitutive wrong in the foundation of democratic order; but Rancière's tort also registers a miscount rather than a specific injury. Or better yet, Rancière's tort registers a miscount as a kind of injury. Because tort occurs before the formal institution of a system of laws, it cannot belong to the order of justice. Tort is political precisely because it is external to what Rancière refers to as the "order of the police": "Politics is generally seen as the set of procedures whereby aggregation and consent of collectives is achieved, the organization of powers, the distribution of places and roles, and the systems for legitimizing the distributions. I propose to give this system of distribution and legitimization another name. I propose to call it *the police*."[68]

Rancière quickly rebuts that "police" doesn't refer to the Althusserian "petty officer"; that is, by police he does not mean an agent of interpellation but rather, a governmental system that, as Michel Foucault reminds us, concerns itself with the "right disposition of things."[69] The claim Rancière sustains throughout *Dis-Agreement*, then, is that "political philosophy" is an agent of the police rather than of politics.[70] He thus reserves the term *politics* "for an extremely determined activity antagonistic to policing: whatever breaks with the tangible configuration whereby parties and parts or lack of them are defined by a presumption that, by definition, has no place in that configuration—that of the part of those who have no part."[71] In so doing, part of his critical project is to delegitimize the political efficacy of neo-Kantian liberalism by aestheticizing it, by pointing to a possible division between democracy and liberalism, and by showing that such a division is the result of a series of operations of power that configure the perceptual field of political experience.

We saw in the previous pages how a neo-Kantian justification of liberal democracies requires the noncoercive institution of procedures for political argument that guide intersubjective communication. Political disputes are legitimate and, indeed, recognizable as "political" when the procedures of justification are followed; in Rawlsian terms, when the burdens of reason are satisfied. The blaberon, however, is the voicing of a wrong that falls on the deaf ears of the police.

These ears are deaf not because they cannot hear but because there are no recognizable procedures by which the dissonant humming of the blaberon may be acknowledged as something other than background noise. Contrasted to the politesse of police deliberation, the political blaberon looks and sounds like a kind of billingsgate, crude and disruptive. "For political philosophy to exist," Rancière explains, "the order of political idealities must be linked to some construction of city 'parts,' to a count whose complexities may mask a fundamental miscount, a miscount that may well be the *blaberon*, the very wrong that is the stuff of politics . . . Politics arises from a count of community 'parts,' which is always a false count, a double count or a miscount."[72] This miscounted element, he goes on to explain, is the divisive "no-part" of "the part of those who have no part": not only a miscounted element within the larger ordering of a polity, but also the ones who have no part in politics—namely, the unrepresentable.

Rancière's image of political thought invokes the kinds of aesthetic features associated with the Burkean sublime. Indeed, for Rancière the democratic sublime that scared both Burke and Bentham generates a politically valuable state of stupor. Political interlocution, Rancière suggests, "has always mixed up language games and rules of expression, and it has always particularized the universal in demonstrative sequences comprised of the meeting of heterogeneous elements."[73] The difficulty in democratic politics, then, is not in determining the causes, effects, and correctives for communicative failure. Rather, "the problem is knowing whether the subjects who count in the interlocution 'are' or 'are not,' whether they are speaking or just making noise."[74] This problem for Rancière is ultimately an aesthetic problem that addresses the configuration of our perceptive competencies: "Politics," he concludes, "is aesthetic in that it makes visible what had been excluded from a perceptual field, and in that it makes audible what used to be inaudible."[75]

Both Rawls and Rancière begin from the condition of disagreement as *the* condition of modern politics. In contrast to Rawls's political calculus of summation, however, Rancière's poetics of political thinking aspires to a mathematical calculus of division. As I argued,

Rawls's commitment to the n + 1 formula of equality corresponds to a commitment to a mimetic model of representation, to the idea that nothing is in and of itself unrepresentable. In contrast, democratic politics exists for Rancière precisely because of the unrepresentable element that is democracy's constitutive feature. Under Rancière's schema, democratic politics is a politics that repeatedly divides itself and, through this endless division, is constantly producing divisive remainders that count as the no-part proper to politics. But to refer to the democratically and politically relevant element as "the part of those who have no part" suggests something more than a poststructural aporia. The "no-part" are, by definition, those who are not ordered: they are the ones without part but they are also the ones without a party. That is, the "no-part" make noises but do not speak; they merely blabber, because they lack representation. Lacking any kind of party affiliation, they literally do not count, and it is this unrepresentable, sublime element that is, for Rancière, the sine qua non of democracy. Politics, then, is distinguishable from the police by a constitutive unrepresentability that interrupts the order of mimesis. "Democracy," he concludes,

> is not the parliamentary system or the legitimate State. It is not a state of the social either, the reign of individualism or the masses. Democracy is, in general, politics' mode of subjectification if, by politics, we mean something other than the organization of bodies as a community and the management of places, powers and functions. *Democracy is more precisely the name of a singular disruption of this order of distribution of bodies as community that we proposed to conceptualize in the broader concept of the police.*[76]

Democracy is the kind of divisive force feared by both Burke and Bentham. It is a disruption of the authority of sociability and history; it is, in short, a transgression that marks a death that is also a birth. To be sure, its disruptive force is not a simple deconstruction of the established order of the police but a break or rupture in the order of things that occasions creative reconfiguration.[77] Contrary to the polite manners of Rawls's deliberative democracy, Rancière's poetics of political thinking is at once rude and base—one might even be tempted to say impolitic. Rancière's privileged image of political thought is one of people speaking out of turn, producing noises, and interrupting those whose turn it is to speak.

In their respective poetics of political thinking, John Rawls and Jacques Rancière present two contrasting accounts of the function of representation in democratic politics. My point in bringing these two authors into conversation with one another is not to highlight their own disagreements; these are evident and require little expository work. Rather, it is to show two distinct approaches to the practice of criticism vis-à-vis political life. What each figure demonstrates, in distinct though not necessarily incommensurate ways, is a simultaneity of aesthetic and moral reasoning when engaged in political thinking. Rawls's image of political thought is redemptive in its commitment to bipartisanship: the critic's role is to restore the beautiful—to suture the ruptures that tear along the texture of a polity. On his rendering, democratic politics is always at risk of dissolution as it anxiously teeters along the edge of constitutional breakdown. The task of political thinking is to provide those exemplary judgments that assist in preventing the dissolution of the beautiful. For Rancière, the democratic moment reveals a sublime tort that constitutes the "crises of judgment" Rawls fears most. His image of political thought tends toward the partisan: accountability is divisive as it exposes a constitutive inequality at the heart of a political system. Equality and tort, then, are principles of political illegitimacy that allow democracy to occur rather than merely persist.

Rawls's and Rancière's images of political thought evince a substantive aesthetic dimension to political argument. A political position or action may be attractive not only because it makes moral sense but also because what allows it to make sense is a spectator's appraisal. The critical difference between these two figures, then, is not found in their ethical commitments to equality: as we have seen, both thinkers start from such a commitment. Rather, the difference between Rawls and Rancière (and, *ceteris paribus*, between a liberal and poststructural image of political thought) lies in a fundamental contention over the referentiality of *the* term of political discourse: namely, politics. This, ultimately, is a contest over what is given to sense perception when making political judgments. The sources of such appraisals go well beyond what the epistemology of argument recommends, and to overlook the aesthetic quality of these sources would be to significantly impoverish the stature of both political theory and criticism.

4

The Force of Political Argument

HABERMAS, HAZLITT, AND THE ESSAY

> If my mind could gain a firm footing, I would not make essays,
> I would make decisions. —MICHEL DE MONTAIGNE

Politic Reading and Writing

Were it possible to reduce methodological disagreements in political theory to one dominant theme, that theme would focus on the status of a literary education in contemporary democracies. Theoretical debates, the liberal/poststructural debate chief among them, presume a commitment to protocols of reading and writing competence that establish boundaries for legitimate forms of discourse. Indeed, the "crisis of interpretation" of the 1980s and 1990s—the nom de plume of the liberal/poststructural debate—is a crisis over postsecondary education.[1] The disciplinary corollary to this crisis is the question of the relative merits of the humanities for the social sciences (and vice versa). How should one read and write? What is subject to interpretation? How are we to educate students so that they might be critically engaged citizens? These ethical questions invoke standards of thinking that constitute an image of what counts as good thought.

Though disagreement persists when answering such methodological questions, a consensus exists regarding the literary genre most amenable to the reading and writing of political argument: the essay, the predominant form of political writing today. The term *essay* comes from the title of Michel de Montaigne's *Essais*; a term famously derived from the French verb *essayer*, meaning *to try*, which, in itself, gives us a good sense of the circumscribed nature of this prosaic form. This species of reflective prose is literally an attempt an author makes to expound upon a particular subject.[2] In the "Epistle to the Reader" of his own *Essay Concerning Understanding*, for instance, John Locke echoes Montaigne's sentiments describing how the *Essay* began from a conversation with "five or six friends meeting at my chamber, discoursing on a subject very remote from this," producing some "hasty and undigested thoughts" that were jotted down, resulting in a "discontinued way of writing."[3] For Locke, as for Montaigne and others, the essay carries with it an attitude of critical responsiveness—a readerly ethos inviting to anyone who reads—but also an opportunity to challenge the lacunas, omissions, and satirical exaggerations of an author.

In this chapter, I explore some difficulties that emerge between the practice of essay writing and the dedication to philosophical argument in contemporary political thought. I begin with a discussion of the essay as a literary genre oriented toward the ill-formed or the incomplete. I then turn to Jürgen Habermas's commitment to the "unforced force of the better argument"[4] solicited to assuage the threat of communicative failure and help guide individuals in reaching understanding. From his arsenal of political criticism, Habermas offers up the performative contradiction, a tool of immanent critique intended to satisfy the demands of clarity that structure both his conception of freedom and his dialogical ethics.[5] I contrast Habermas's account of political argument with that of William Hazlitt, a nineteenth-century writer who takes advantage of the fragmentary nature of the essay in order to represent his radical democratic imaginary. Hazlitt's writings show how human truths are far from confined to the genre of philosophical justification, thereby providing a more capacious account of political thinking, one more associable with the experiences of self-contradiction and discursive interruption characteristic of democratic life.

A Discontinued Way of Writing

The word *grotesque* first appears in English as *grotesco* in John Florio's translation of Montaigne's *Essays* (1632). It is a classical term of art that derives from the Italian *grotta*, meaning cave. *Grotesco* literally means "of the cave" and refers to a style of painting found in ancient Roman caverns (first discovered during the excavation of Titus's baths) consisting of "representations of portions of human and animal forms, fantastically combined and interwoven with foliage and flowers."[6] From the medieval period through to the Renaissance, the grotesque intermingling of forms came to symbolize motifs of regeneration and the human condition of mutability. "There was no longer the movement of finished forms, vegetable or animal, in a finished and stable world," explains Mikhail Bakhtin. "Instead, the inner movement of being itself was expressed in the passing of one form into the other, in the ever incomplete character of being."[7]

Language was not immune from this incessant play of admixtures, and neither was literary composition. Michel de Montaigne starts his essay "Of Friendship" invoking the tradition of the grotesque to describe the art of the essay. "Having considered the proceedings of a painter that serves me," he begins, "I had in mind to imitate his ways."[8] The term *imitation* alerts us to the import of what Montaigne is about to write. In the early modern aesthetic imaginary, one imitates greatness (*grandezza*) in all its guises. But this instance of imitation is also a kind of perversion that coincides with the subject of his imitative proclivities. He continues: "He [the painter] chooses the fairest place and middle of any wall, or panel, wherein to draw a picture, which he finishes with his outmost care and art, and the vacuity about it he fills with grotesques, which are odd fantastic figures without any grace but what they derive from their variety, and the extravagance of their shapes." At first glance grotesques might appear simply decorative, their function limited to filling up space.

However, we know that there was anxiety regarding vacant spaces in the period, as I suggested in chapter 2. The purpose of the grotesque, then, was not only decorative but also psychological: it was intended to protect spectators from a generalized fear of nothingness often associated with an Augustinian view of evil and a denial of God's ultimate goodness.[9] Montaigne's admiration for his painter's grotesquery carries with it a refusal of nihilism and a commitment to the regenerative forces of a world of becoming. Ultimately, Montaigne imitates this through writing: "And in truth," he asks in the last sentence of this introductory paragraph, "what are these things I scribble, other than grotesque and monstrous bodies, made up of various parts, without any certain figure or any other than accidental order, coherence, or proportion?"[10]

Rather than painting, then, Montaigne chooses to imitate by using an alternative and novel art form he describes as a grotesque scribble with no direction or purpose to it: namely, the essay. It would be a mistake, I think, to conclude that Montaigne is being falsely modest, or even ironic, in his account of the art of the essay. He does not intend his comments about the monstrous and incomplete character of this innovative genre negatively. Coupled with the insight that the playfulness of the grotesque rescues us from a kind of nihilism that imagines death as an insurmountable nothingness, the genre of the essay comes to possess all the qualities of becoming that Bakhtin attributes to early modern grotesque imagery. By imitating grotesque painting through essay writing, Montaigne makes the essay's piecemeal nature its grandezza.

Yet Montaigne's appreciation of the grotesque's grandezza not only informs his theory of composition, it also speaks to an ethics of reading. Notice the extent to which his description of the painter focuses on the latter's movements, how he proceeds from the center, outward. The beautiful object is placed in the middle of the wall, and the "vacuity about" is filled with grotesques. As much as this is an account of an artistic technique, it is also a phenomenology of perspective, an account of the experience of movement through perception. The grotesque demands a centrifugal reading strategy, one that does not look for the kernel of meaning within a closed system but rather, moves outward and away from the center. Insisting on the difficulty of certainty, Montaigne ultimately asserts, "If my mind could gain a firm footing, I would not make essays, I would make decisions; but it is always in apprenticeship and on trial."[11] Montaigne's scribbles, then, are not only an example of the grotesque, they also demand a grotesque mindset: The essay is centrifugal by nature, and as such, it commands a readerly ethos attuned to the dispersions of a fantastical world of becoming.

That the essay possesses the quality of becoming does not mean that it does not have form. Rather, as Montaigne's scribbles make abundantly clear, incoherence and disproportion constitute the form of the essay as a literary genre. Theodor Adorno expands on this point when he contrasts the form of the essay to a discursive logic characterized by theoretical continuity and coherence. Insisting, as Montaigne did, on the tentative character of the essayer, Adorno concludes that "discontinuity is essential to the essay; its subject matter is always a conflict brought to a standstill. While the essay coordinates concepts with one another by means of their function in the parallelogram of forces in its objects," he continues, "it shrinks from any overarching concept to which they could all be subordinated."[12] Here the essay possesses an inherently contradictory attitude. Though it is not committed to being "unlogical"—in that "no mere contradictions may remain unless they are established as belonging to the object itself"[13]—the essay nonetheless operates on a principle of composition that refuses the a priori imperative of philosophical coherence. In this respect, Adorno asserts, "the essay reflects what is loved and hated instead of presenting the mind as a creation *ex nihilo* on the model of an unrestrained work ethic. Luck and play are essential to it. It starts not with Adam and Eve but with what it wants to talk about; it says what occurs to it in that context and stops when it feels finished rather than when there is nothing to say."[14] Everything about the form of the essay is mundane. Essay writing begins in medias res; it is a genre of writing committed to life in that its sources of inspiration are the experiences of living creatures. In this respect, the essay is "the critical form par excellence";[15] it is a mundane art form because its objective is to be critically engaged with the world around it. It is mundane also because the essay repudiates both the conclusiveness of a post-Enlightenment model of scientific rationality and the metaphysics of origins of philosophical discourse. Instead, the essay's formal commitment to becoming favors an associational logic of cross-connections between disparate and diverse elements.

The essay thus lends itself best to representing a world of monstrous copulations: its innermost formal law, Adorno concludes, is heresy: "Through violations of the orthodoxy of thought, something in the object [of reflection] becomes visible which it is orthodoxy's secret and objective aim to keep invisible."[16] This heretical feature helps explain why the essay became such an important form of writing during the height of the democratic revolutions of the eighteenth century. One literary scholar notes how "essays are organized by a horizontal structure of "conversation," a mutually defining relationship between two agents, and they offer an alternative structure to that of law, to the relationship between subject and law."[17] Indeed, by adhering to a transgressive logic of becoming, the form of the essay repudiates the hierarchical architectonic of power characteristic of the logic of sovereignty. There is thus an ethics to this aesthetics of political writing that contemporary accounts of the nature of political argument, committed to the language game of philosophical justification, overlook. By attending to these features we recognize a mode of writing best adaptable to a political imaginary that appreciates the manner in which the limits of representation characteristic of democratic life are not a sign of institutional failure but are, rather, the conditions of possibility for critical engagement and political action.

The Value of Sincerity

Jürgen Habermas's project of a discourse theory of ethics is an attempt at establishing norms of critical judgment for everyday communication. His theory of communicative action—committed, as it is, to a rationalist account of intersubjective engagement—appropriates from the hermeneutic/phenomenological tradition of Edmund Husserl and Hans-Georg Gadamer the concept of the "lifeworld," deriving from it rules that permit participants to reach understanding. Habermas's principal aim is immanent critique: to show how the lifeworld—"a storehouse of unquestioned cultural givens"[18]—is comprised of differentiable value spheres, aesthetic, moral, and scientific, each of which contains distinct sources for validity claims.

From this vantage point Habermas's model of argumentative exchange is inherently agonistic: "What moral theory can do, and should be trusted to do," he states, "is clarify the universal core of our moral intuitions and thereby refute value skepticism."[19] As we shall soon see, "trust" is a core value in this project. Individuals possess faculties like a will and an intellect that find their highest form of expression through the practices of refutation and clarification. Political thinking is virtuous, then, when a subject uses argument to convince others of the legitimacy of their position. Because persuasion cannot rely on coercion, communicative participants must trust the neutral force of the better argument to function as the agent of conviction. Furthermore, competence requires an understanding of the world that includes (a) the skill to differentiate between diverse modes of thinking and (b) an ability to apply the proper form of judgment to each domain of thought. Habermas specifies three types of validity claims,[20] each of which corresponds to a responsive attitude. If we were to add a forth category to this schema—modes of reasoning—we would see that the tripartite division of "truth, rightness, and taste" corresponds to Immanuel Kant's division of pure, practical, and aesthetic reason. As much has been written on Habermas's treatment of the first two categories of thinking, I focus on the last: aesthetic reason. Habermas's image of political thinking carries with it a tacit aesthetic dimension that is hidden in the larger, procedural aspects of his theoretical writings.

Consider the following claim. "Agreement in the communicative practice of everyday life," asserts Habermas, "rests simultaneously on intersubjective shared propositional knowledge, on normative accord, and on mutual trust."[21] Habermas spends a considerable amount of time discussing how propositional knowledge and normative accord are amenable to consensus, but he never explains why it is that consensus ought to be the goal of communicative exchange. To put

Domains of Thought	Classes of Speech Acts	Domains of Focus
cognitive	constative	truth
interactive	regulative	rightness (justice)
expressive	representative	sincerity (taste)

the matter slightly differently, Habermas's discussion of communicative action eschews an extended treatment of the value of sincerity or mutual trust. Yet sincerity (or trust/truthfulness) is a tacit condition of intersubjective participation: we must be sincere in our desire for consensus, we must be sincere when speaking, and we must be sincere in our critical commitment to philosophical justification. Most important, however, individuals must be sincere and truthful when exercising power: "Agreement," Habermas declares, "cannot be imposed or brought about by manipulating one's partner in interaction, for something that patently owes its existence to external pressure cannot even be considered an agreement."[22] The most striking thing about this last statement is not its commitment to a form of discourse that is entirely uncoercive and hence free (although, as many have remarked, this is a problematic feature of Habermas's argument);[23] rather, it is the manner in which mutual trust is a structural and tacit (by which I mean unacknowledged) feature of an ethics of communication. Participants engage in discourse not only to satisfy the rationalist condition of attaining understanding and agreement but also because they trust that others involved in this scenario will neither strong-arm them into submission nor turn back on their commitments.[24] In this regard, the "truthfulness" or "sincerity" (what guarantees mutual trust) appropriate to the domain of the aesthetic is both a specific type of validity claim *and* an important attribute in the making and redeeming of validity claims in general. This means that an issue about truthfulness (and trust) can erupt in the midst of any sort of discourse as so happens, for example, when participants are charged with performative contradiction.

Discourse ethics presupposes tacit principles that treat argument as the most appropriate mode of political engagement. The performative contradiction is one such process that stands as a procedural norm for the critical analysis of speech utterances. It may thus be conceived both positively (as a principle guaranteeing noncoercive communication) and negatively (as an indirect means of corrective training for speech participants). Seyla Benhabib explains how the performative contradiction is a recent addition to Habermas's critical arsenal, borrowed from Karl-Otto Apel's attempt to counteract the moral skeptic. Her formulation is worth quoting at length:

> Apel uses this argument to establish two propositions: first, the skeptic who doubts that it is possible to rationally settle validity claims gets involved in a performative contradiction; for to raise such a claim she must participate in an argumentation which itself is impossible without the assumption that disputed claims can be rationally settled. Second, Apel thus wants to maintain that the cognitive as well as the moral skeptic must recognize that the situation is an "unavoidable" and "uncircumventible" condition of the very possibility of speech acts.... Thus cognitive and moral skeptics who deny that valid normative claims can be established at all, through the very fact that they raise a validity claim to be settled argumentatively, commit themselves to the normative ideal of a community of communication.

With respect to Habermas's position, Benhabib explains that "whereas formerly Habermas asked whether the conditions of an ideal speech situation *entailed* the acceptance of certain ethical norms, he is now asking whether all subjects capable of speech and action, in that they act communicatively, do not also dispose of a certain moral know-how which involves recognizing a certain moral principle which they can deny at the risk of a *performative contradiction* only."[25] This explanation rightly insists on the tacit dimension of this principle. The performative contradiction is a moral norm built into the structure of communication and, as such, asserts its normative status when thinking goes awry. Habermas's discourse ethics thus attempts to reconstruct the norms of accountability that govern everyday communication and promote freedom. "Subjects engaged in communicative action orient themselves to validity claims," he explains. Further:

> This is why there is no form of sociocultural life that is not at least implicitly geared to maintaining communicative action by means of

argument.... That is why the radical skeptic's refusal to argue is an empty gesture. No matter how consistent a dropout he may be, he cannot drop out of the communicative practice of everyday life, to the presuppositions of which he remains bound. And these in turn are at least partly identical with the presuppositions of argumentation as such.[26]

Irony is the mood of the performative contradiction: it asserts that the stated meaning of an argument (i.e., that there are no a priori norms) is the opposite of that expressed by the speech act itself (i.e., by asserting the absence of a priori norms, one is actually instituting a norm). Yet there is something more at stake here than the question of epistemological validity. By making the performative contradiction an element of what, with Michael Polanyi, we may call "tacit knowing,"[27] Habermas also makes it a standard of legitimacy for successful interaction between and among individuals. In order to speak properly and have what they say be valid, individuals are required to speak as though they are telling the truth of themselves in public. This recurring kernel of sincerity that qualifies a discourse theory of ethics also presumes that when I speak, I do so with the promissory obligation that what I say is an accurate representation of what I think, meaning that what I say is the truth of my self. By putting their cards on the table and not holding anything back, so to speak, participants satisfy the tacit condition of truthfulness (imposed by the performative contradiction) and thus engage in communicative, rather than strategic, action.

Habermas's recent adoption of the performative contradiction thus presents us with a state of truth telling that transforms the res publica (the public thing) into a *res putatio* (a cleansed thing); or rather, makes it so that the res publica may persist if and only if individuals speak the truth of themselves. There is a confluence here of an aesthetic and moral vision that governs sociopolitical interaction. If the performative contradiction is to give us an ideal image of what is to count as a "good" thought, then the virtuous individual must be the one who does not speak in contradictions. To use words incorrectly, to speak out of turn, to not say what one means—all of these obstacles to successful communication force us to doubt an other's reputation; and, as Habermas makes clear in his historical narrative of the rise of the bourgeois public sphere, the building of trust through reputation—"what one represents in the opinion of others"[28]—is precisely what is at stake in the condition of sincerity.

Importantly, the twin aesthetic and political dimensions of the performative contradiction find their historical grounding in an eighteenth-century "principle of publicity." This principle first arose out of the domain of aesthetic criticism that was, explicitly, a private attempt to undermine the authoritarian power structure of aristocratic and monarchical rule. The "literary precursor" to the bourgeois public sphere is the first to ground its critical authority on the force of the better argument: "The art critics could see themselves as spokesmen for the public—and in their battles with the artists this was the central slogan—because they knew of no authority beside that of the better argument and because they felt themselves at one with all those who were willing to let themselves be convinced by better arguments."[29] At first glance, the appeal to "the authority of the better argument" seems uncontroversial, especially if we consider that the pedagogical curriculum for most art critics of the period would have included schooling in the ars rhetorica. Overlooking the tradition of rhetoric altogether, however, Habermas wants the authoritative force of the better argument to count as something other than a tried and true humanist skill. For it to have the valence and legitimacy it requires, "argument" must be more weighty, from a moral point of view: to be a politically relevant mode of critical engagement, argument needs to produce ethically significant truth-claims, where "ethical" here refers to a sense of *Sittlichkeit* that imbues Habermas's conception of the lifeworld.[30]

A commitment to argument thus builds community. Art critics felt themselves at one with those with whom they could argue, not only because these individuals might have something in common—the object of their criticism—but also because they had a form of interaction in common: argumentation. The rise of this novel style of engagement also marks a shift in power relations. Rather than depending on absolutist rule, where the master (whether prince, nobleman, or monarch) instructs as to what is right or wrong, good taste or bad, these individual "spokesmen for the public" imagined themselves immune from such circumscriptions by the simple fact that they were arguing—that is, by the simple fact that they were reasoning in public. As exemplary participants in public reason, Habermas concludes, these individuals offered the public at large a participationist form of power, egalitarian in that anyone who could use their right reason correctly could participate, and democratically agonistic in that it challenged the political structure of authoritarian, aristocratic rule. Thus reason was able to "shed its dependence on the authority of the aristocratic noble hosts and to acquire that autonomy that turns conversation into criticism and *bons mots* into arguments."[31]

This stylistic contrast between (polite) conversation and (contestatory) argument in Habermas's conception of democratic criticism begs further scrutiny. Admirable is the implication that criticism, by its very nature, is a form of political action. The eighteenth-century art critic's attempt to explain their judgment of taste by the force of the better argument counts, for Habermas, as a form of protest against authoritarian rule. Such instances of contestation found their home in the proliferation of popular journals like those of Joseph Addison and Richard Steele. It was in these publications that a general public could evaluate an image of itself; that is, witness and critique itself through aesthetic representation: "In the *Tatler*, the *Spectator*, and the *Guardian*," Habermas claims, "the public held up a mirror to itself. . . . The public that read and debated about this sort of thing read and debated about itself."[32] These essayistic journals and literary precursors to the public sphere represented to the public an image of good criticism;[33] that is, the image in the mirror the public holds up to itself is the ideal of communication as argument.

This is the promise of "democratic criticism" Habermas discovers in the bourgeois public sphere. The contemporary corollary to this is the performative contradiction, a concept whose principal value lies in deriving a polemical image of engagement that exemplifies "good thought" and is not coercive. By making a strong distinction between conversation and argument and by encoding onto that distinction corresponding relations of power (conversation/aristocratic domination vs. argument/democratic autonomy), however, Habermas renders debate in a democratic order into a form that corresponds to a tight model of argument. Dialogue and conversation cannot count within this democratic aesthetic because of the threat of contradiction and coercion implied by the formal features Habermas attributes to these styles of engagement.

Rather than dialogical, Habermas's model of communicative action starts to look surprisingly monological. Though it is not absolutist in principle, the aesthetic features of communicative action allow only one possible mode of successful communication: argument. The alternative is contradiction and miscomprehension—an alternative that is, by its very nature, anathema to Habermas's understanding of communicative action as "the unforced force of the better argument [that] determines the 'yes' or 'no' responses of the participants."[34]

Ultimately, the charge of having "performed a contradiction" is polemical to the extent that it does not invite a response but declares the senselessness of an utterance and the untrustworthy character of the speaker. Ensconced in this charge is a commitment to the apodictic stature of philosophical justification, a commitment that is beyond argument because it grounds the possibility for argument. But could it not be the case that something ethically and/or politically valuable is lost when we demand that the subjects of communication be, above all else, *sincere* (by which I also mean coherent)? William Hazlitt's essays provide one possible answer to this question.

William Hazlitt's Familiar Style

Habermas regrets ignoring the relevance of a plebeian public sphere in his study of bourgeois publicity. He confesses that "only after reading Mikhail Bakhtin's great book *Rabelais and His World* have my eyes become really opened to the inner dynamics of a plebeian culture. This culture of the common people was by no means only a backdrop, that is, a passive echo of the dominant culture; it was also the periodically recurring violent revolt of a counterproject to the hierarchical world of domination, with its official celebrations and everyday disciplines."[35] Having said this, Habermas still maintains the distinction between high and low culture that structures his original refusal to examine plebeian publicity.³⁶ Specifically citing the London Jacobins as an example, Habermas concludes that "the exclusion of the culturally and politically mobilized lower strata entails a pluralization of the public sphere in the very process of its emergence. Next to, and interlocked with, the hegemonic public sphere, a plebeian one assumes shape."³⁷

In the last decade of the eighteenth century, the themes of regeneration and renovation were on the minds of poets, philosophers, and politicians alike. "Bliss was it in that dawn to be alive," wrote William Wordsworth in *The Prelude*. There was an intoxication in the air that promised, with the birth of the spirit of liberty, that anything was possible. Such enthusiasm was quickly buttressed as the decade came to an end. The optimism declared by the philosophers of perfectibility (chief among them Jean-Jacques Rousseau, the "father" of romanticism)³⁸ was tempered when revolutionary fervor transformed itself into revolutionary terror. "Political life in France after 1789," one scholar notes, "had been less like a neo-classical drama which respected individual agency and personal integrity and more of a grotesque popular carnival beyond the control of public authority."³⁹ Certainly this is what Edmund Burke fears in his *Reflections on the Revolution in France*, and this vision continues to be shared by many thinkers to this day. But for writers at the turn of the century, the 1790s proved to be a contradictory time that waxed and waned between liberty and libertinage. Indeed, much intellectual energy was spent in trying to at once embrace the spirit of liberty and repudiate its unseemly heritage, to disavow the revolutionary legacy while attempting to redeem it.⁴⁰

With the turn of the century, an expression attributed to a speech delivered in 1800 by William Pitt gained currency in England: "Once a Jacobin, always a Jacobin." *Jacobin* was an easy way of expressing abuse against one's adversaries. It referred to an immediately suspect attitude or stance that stood as a reliable typological category of immanent danger (perhaps it still does). Addressing this expression in a *Morning Post* essay (October 21, 1802), Samuel Taylor Coleridge redeems the term. He proceeds negatively, describing what the different sects of anti-Jacobins mean by it. Surprisingly, he classifies himself in the "third class" who use the word for lack of a better term but also believe there are definite ideas attached to it. "A Jacobin, in *our* sense of the term," he explains,

> is one who believes, and is disposed to act on the belief, that all, or the greater part of, the happiness or misery, virtue or vice, of mankind, depends on forms of government; who admits no form of government is either good or rightful, which does not flow directly and formally from the persons governed; who—considering life, health, moral and intellectual improvement, and liberty both of person and conscience, as blessings which governments are bound as far as possible to increase and secure to every inhabitant, whether he has or has not any fixed property, and moreover as blessings of infinitely greater value to each individual, then the preservation of property can be to any individual—does consequently and consistently hold, that every inhabitant, that has attained the age of reason, has a natural and inalienable right to an *equal* share of power in the choice of the governors. In other words, the Jacobin affirms that no legislature can be rightful or good, which did not proceed from universal suffrage.[41]

No longer a term of abuse, *Jacobin* is reconfigured as a signifier for universal suffrage. At once, it retains the force of a radical participatory democracy that encourages equality by any means necessary— whether revolutionary, rebellious, or even criminal under the laws of "faulty governments." The Jacobin imaginary Coleridge describes involves reasoned principles of good government, a commitment to an ethics of representation, and an unbridled enthusiasm for political action. A Jacobin is, in short, a potential agent of disturbance whose participationist concerns are at the heart of his or her critical practices.

William Hazlitt shared this Jacobin imaginary with Coleridge. Born the son of a prominent Unitarian minister in England (1778), Hazlitt spent part of his childhood in Boston (1783–87), where his father established the first Unitarian Church in the United States. Upon his return to England, he attended the New College at Hackney until 1795, when he decided that he no longer wanted to follow in his father's footsteps. That summer, he joined his brother in London, immersing himself in the thriving intellectual culture of early-nineteenth-century England. There he began his philosophical pursuits, reading widely in the English poets, Burke, and Rousseau. While lecturing on a wide variety of issues, including philosophy, politics, and drama, he published his first book: a philosophical inquiry titled *An Essay on the Principles of Human Action* (1805). In the second decade of the 1800s, he became best known for his journalism and his dramatic and literary criticism, publishing *Characters of Shakespeare's Plays* (1817) and *Political Essays* (1819).

Jean-Jacques Rousseau was the modern author Hazlitt most admired, but it was the Rousseau of *The Confessions*, rather than of the political writings, that he appreciated most. In *The Confessions* Rousseau expands upon his conception of human experience, an exposition Hazlitt found lacking in modern philosophy. He made a virtue of Rousseau's egoism by showing its relevance to the concept of sympathy. Gregory Dart explains:

> In order for someone to be behaving selfishly, Hazlitt reasoned, they would have to be acting in the interest of their future self, a self which had not, strictly speaking, yet come into being, whose conditions and circumstances were not yet known, and whose very existence was, in a sense, very imaginary. But if a man was able to sympathize with an imaginary future self, then surely he was also capable of sympathizing with another present self, that is, another person, for such an effort of sympathy would involve exactly the same kind of self-projection.[42]

Hazlitt used this version of sympathy to attack Benthamite reforms by soliciting the essay's very form as evidence of Bentham's intellectual failures. The essay represented a means by which readers might at once form sympathies and antipathies with what is written, and the ability to engage in such a reading strategy was, for Hazlitt, a chief indication of the limits of Benthamite Utilitarianism. To explain: rather than a conception of human agency and social organization that directed governmental institutions to collect the mass of diverse human preferences into a representable whole, in the essay Hazlitt engages readers to appraise their own experiences of attachment and detachment by insisting on the limits of representation as a condition of democratic life.[43]

Hazlitt's oeuvre comprises twenty-one volumes, including a collection of essays titled *The Plain Speaker* (1826). The title is indicative of the kind of conversational style of engagement Hazlitt imagines as characteristic of the essay. In this book, Hazlitt presents himself conversing on a variety of topics (envy, hatred, egotism, genius), self-consciously echoing Montaigne's essays, for which he held the highest regard.[44] But the "plain speaker" is not merely conversing; he also speaks (and writes) a "familiar style" that is neither "vulgar" nor "pompous."[45] The literariness of an essay is synonymous with what Hazlitt calls "common conversation." When composing an essay, then, the author must value a word not for its meaning but for its use: "The proper force of words," he explains, "lies not in the words themselves but in their application."[46] Continuing from this general principle, Hazlitt asserts, not without some dramatic verve, that he "hate[s] anything that occupies more space than it is worth. I hate to see a load of band-boxes go along the street, and I hate to see a parcel of big words without anything in them."[47] Through these criticisms we begin to see how Hazlitt's theory of composition informs his larger critical horizon: His commitment to the familiar style of the plain speaker sources his political objections to the utilitarians of his day, Jeremy Bentham and Thomas Malthus chief among them. Especially, with regards to the latter, Hazlitt will attack his rhetorical use of calculations—those "paper bullets of the brain"[48]—that presume to be inherently meaningful but whose real function is to confound readers into submission. In contrast, Hazlitt will use a familiar style to counteract the aggregating tendencies of statistical flourishes. Especially in his *What Is the People?* essay, Hazlitt generates endless descriptive lists of "the people." This he does not in order to provide an exhaustive definition of his topic, but rather to show that the inexhaustibility of a people's descriptive features cannot be contained by mathematical formulae.

Commentators remark on Hazlitt's exemplary ability to move freely from one perspective to the next. David Bromwich notes that

"Hazlitt's essays communicate the author's tact for shifting inclinations, for negotiating between . . . different *languages* of action."[49] Indeed, Hazlitt insists that the imagination and the sentiments, crucial to the writing of essays, motivate action. This experience is expressed most poignantly in one of his *Political Essays*, where he exclaims that "to be a true Jacobin a man must be a good hater; but this is the most difficult and least amiable of all the virtues: the most trying and the most thankless of all tasks. The love of liberty consists in the hatred of tyrants."[50] As free-floating of a signifier "Jacobinism" may be, for Hazlitt it encompassed a sympathy for the revolutionary ideal of liberty and an antipathy toward authoritarian rule. This constitutive tension between sympathy and antipathy is poignantly displayed in one of his most provocative and enticing essays dedicated to the pleasure of hating.

Hatred is a distasteful sentiment, and to make this a principle of democratic action may seem, at first glance, excessive; especially given certain contemporary proclivities for a "politics of friendship." But Hazlitt understands hatred in a unique way and, in "The Pleasure of Hating," he proceeds to elaborate the value of this sentiment for political criticism. He begins by specifying how hatred does not imply a desire to harm but rather is a natural sentiment born of our imagination:

> There is a spider crawling along the matted floor of the room where I sit (not the one which has been so well allegorized in the admirable *Lines to a Spider*; but another of the same edifying breed)—he runs with heedless, hurried haste, he hobbles awkwardly towards me, he stops—he sees the giant shadow before him, and, at a loss whether to retreat or to proceed, meditates his huge foe—but as I do not start up and seize upon the straggling caitiff, as he would upon a hapless fly within his toils, he takes heart, and ventures on, with mingled cunning, impudence, and fear.[51]

A mundane occurrence, to see a spider walk across one's rug. But with characteristic elegance, the scene is transformed into the epitome of confrontation. Two mighty forces: on the one hand, the spider that invokes "mystic horror and superstitious loathing" and, on the other, Hazlitt's shadow—"a huge foe." Of course, Hazlitt comes off the better of the two, as he chooses not to squash the spider, whereas he knows very well that if the spider were in the same position with "a hapless fly," generosity would not be its virtue. There is, then, a contradiction in his relation to the spider. By not crushing it, Hazlitt at once sympathizes with the spider—he understands the spider's impulse to consume a hapless fly—and despises it for being such an odious creature. Though the simultaneity of sympathy and antipathy may differ from Habermas's understanding of contradiction in philosophical argument, the sense of unsettledness that arises from the structure of contradiction is similar and the impulse to resolve the tension is, for Hazlitt, counterproductive.

Hazlitt's refusal to respond violently suggests that the size of the shadow (the "huge foe") does not represent merely the dimensions of Hazlitt's body but perhaps also indicates the stature of his character. He is too much of a "good hater" to crush the creature; instead, he will write of his disgust. He continues:

> A child, a woman, a clown, or a moralist a century ago, would have crushed the little reptile to death—my philosophy has got beyond that—I bear the creature no ill-will, but still I hate the very sight of it. The spirit of malevolence survives the practical exertion of it. We learn to curb our will and keep our overt actions within the bounds of humanity, long before we can subdue our sentiments and imaginations to the same mild tone. We give up the external demonstration, the *brute* violence, but cannot part with the essence or principle of hostility.[52]

Hazlitt makes an important distinction between hatred and contempt: He might hate the spider, but he bears it no ill will; that is, his philosophy has surpassed the impulse to condemn the arachnid for being a spider. Also significant is the shift from the first person singular to the plural *we*, as it points to a general claim Hazlitt will sustain regarding human beings as such: humans are incoherent and contradictory creatures; the imagination fuels these contradictions, and these contradictions sustain life. "Nature seems (the more we look into it) made up of antipathies," he explains in the second paragraph of the essay. "Without something to hate, we should loose the very spring of thought and action. Life would turn to a stagnant pool, were it not ruffled by the jarring interests, the unruly passions of men."[53] Such strong passions fuel those energies that make us think and act; humans require such instances of hostility.

Hazlitt's reflections move from the general to the particular, illustrating how hatred is a part of our quotidian existence: "We hate old friends: we hate old books: we hate old opinions; and at last we come to hate ourselves."[54] Cynical though such phrases may seem, it is important to keep in mind the extent to which, for Hazlitt, "hate" is conceived positively as a motivating principle of thought and action. To proceed from a hatred of friends, books, and opinions to a hatred of ourselves means that we, too, are not immune from our own criticisms and from the disdain of others. The self-reflection that may bring about hatred of our selves, like Hazlitt's understanding of the Rousseauian self, is future oriented: it fosters a desire to change. Such self-directed alterations inevitably bring about further changes in allegiances, friendships, and familiar circles: "Old friendships are like meats served up repeatedly," he exclaims, "cold, comfortless, and distasteful. The stomach turns against them."[55]

These passages make Hazlitt look like a nineteenth-century equivalent of a disgruntled postal employee. But it is worth noting that such expressions of distaste are not merely the result of a sociability gone awry, nor are they simply signs of a deep-rooted misanthropy. Hazlitt was both a great lover and a devoted hater. The distaste he felt for old friendships was a reasonable response to changes in one's life, one's social setting, and one's own self. For Hazlitt, the perpetually altering self—constantly exposed to new experiences—becomes a microcosm for the vibrancy of democratic life. Consider the following account of portrait painting:

> The human face is not one thing, as the vulgar suppose, nor does it remain always the same. It has infinite varieties, which the artist is obliged to notice and to reconcile, or he will make strange work. Not only the light and shade upon it do not continue for two minutes the same: the position of the head constantly varies, each feature is in mo-

tion every moment, even while the artist is working at it, and in the course of a day the whole expression of the countenance undergoes a change . . . You can only bring it back again to the same point or give it a consistent construction by an effort of imagination, or a strong feeling of character; and you must connect features together less by the eye than by the mind.[56]

Thematically reminiscent of Montaigne's essay "Of Experience,"[57] this passage allows for an easy substitution of a person's face for the body politic more generally. That the human face has infinite varieties and is in perpetual motion parallels Hazlitt's own description of the people in other essays[58] and, just as the artist must exercise his imagination in order to give a face a "consistent construction," so too must the political actor rely on an equally strenuous imaginative effort— or, indeed, a "strong character"—to provide a tentatively consistent representation of political life.

This passage occasions such a relatively easy substitution also because of its appreciation of the limits of representation. Significant for Hazlitt, however, is not simply that there is an aporetic failure of representation at the heart of any artistic project, but furthermore, that the artist is not distressed by such failures and perseveres, countering the pulsating flow of the blood with his own deft suppleness of the wrist. The constantly altering self, represented here by the lady in the Vandyke portrait, is the same self that can at once sympathize with the spider and hate it all the more—which is to say, it is the same self that experiences the simultaneity of disgust and sympathy by imagining old friendships like meats served up repeatedly.

Hazlitt is well aware that he is not immune from an other's hostility. His life as a journalist and political and literary critic is sufficient testament to this. But he does not disparage such hostilities. Rather, he recounts with admiration how antipathy has shaped the course of his own life. In an appendix to "On the Conversation of Authors," Hazlitt tells of his Thursday night meetings at Charles Lamb's home, where "wit and good fellowship was the motto inscribed over the door."[59] Though this may have been the case, such "good fellowship" expressed itself in curiously antipathetic ways. Hazlitt's description of two of his colleagues is exemplary in this regard: "There was Rickman, who asserted some incredible matter of fact as a likely paradox, and settled the controversy like and *ipse dixit*, a *fiat* of his will, hammering out many a hard theory on the anvil of his brain—the Baron Munchausen of politics and practical philosophy: there was Captain Burney, who had you at an advantage by never understanding you."[60] Upon reading such lines, the reader cannot help but feel something of the disputes at hand; we are invited to imagine who our own "Baron Munchausens of politics and practical philosophy" may be; perhaps we recognize ourselves in the figures of Rickman or Captain Burney. Such jugglings of sympathy and antipathy, investment and detachment mark Hazlitt's attempt to provide, in the essay, a conversational mode of engagement that arises out of the ambivalences and uncertainties of everyday life. Pace Habermas, such conversations neither have the glimmer of aristocratic polite society nor do they imply an authoritarian form of power. At the same time, these conversations do not simply involve the exposition of arguments that one may or may not refute by invoking the performative contradiction. They are disputes that arise from the condition of associating with others; they might fill you with disgust for the person who supports a particular position, but there is no necessary logic at the heart of such distaste. Rather, these antipathies originate from the suddenness of thought, perhaps in response to an other's anvil-like assertions, or the crawling of a spider.

The site of critical concern to which Hazlitt returns is *legitimacy*, a word he repeatedly pens in vitriol rather than ink. Specifically referring to monarchical government, the word also represents the apotheosis of illegitimate power: it is "a detestable fiction, which would make you and me and all mankind its slaves or victims; which would, of right and with all the sanctions of religion and morality, sacrifice the lives of millions to the least of its caprices; which subjects the rights, the happiness, and liberty of nations, to the will of some of the lowest of the species."[61] In such passages, Hazlitt not only attacks renewed attempts to establish divine right succession, but also expresses a critical attitude consonant with his radical democratic imaginary. Such an attitude, epitomized in his excursus on hating, is a provocation of dissensus that finds sustenance in the persistent simultaneity of coexisting dissimilars characteristic of democratic life. From Hazlitt's perspective, political action is necessarily partisan and democratic criticism is intensely polemical.

Contemporary theoretical commitments to satisfying the demands of clarity overlook this properly litigious element of democratic life.[62] Habermas's adoption of philosophic justification as the form of political argument par excellence makes a virtue of bipartisanship by assuming that democratic politics is disposed toward communicative convergence. On this rendering, political argument needs to be cleansed of any murkiness, cognitive, linguistic, or otherwise. But among the many purifying questions that discourse ethics resolves, one question remains unasked: Is it reasonable to assume that a political assertion ought to have—or indeed does have—the same character as a knowledge claim?

Discussing eighteenth- and nineteenth-century literacy, Don Herzog notes a shift in the political effectivity of essays. "The *Tatler*'s decorous ironies," he explains, "depended on the belief that those coffeehouse discussions were merely laughable, that nothing could come of them. But after the Revolution, it was harder to believe that."[63] In his poignant criticism of men, ideas, and political practices, William Hazlitt took advantage of the potentially dangerous and inevitably disruptive opportunities resultant from an essay's laughable ironies, demonstrating how the dissolution of allegiances between individuals, groups, and social orders is crucial to democratic life. Attention to such instances of interruption provides sustenance for novel sources of critical engagement that contemporary accounts of the nature of political argument, with their emphases on the epistemology of argument, ultimately overlook.

Afterword: *Les Sans Papiers*

NO VOX POPULI, VOX DEI

> To affirm the nature of the "poetic" in politics means to assert first and foremost that politics is an activity of reconfiguration of that which is given in the sensible. —JACQUES RANCIÈRE

On March 28, 1996, several hundred foreign workers occupied the Church of St. Ambroise in Paris. The motivation was simple: to become visible and audible. The gesture was symbolic: it evoked the papal nuncio's right of sanctuary. First established in the fifth century, the sanctuary laws state that when someone seeks asylum in a holy or sacred place, they are protected from political persecution.[1] The occupants of St. Ambroise were seeking asylum because they had recently become undocumented, and hence illegal, under new French immigration law.

These laws, known as the Pasqua Laws and named after their proponent (Interior Minister Charles Pasqua), were enacted in 1993 in order to curb the influx of illegal immigration into France from its former colonies in Africa and Asia. Included in these measures were stricter visa requirements, a "zero immigration" policy, and an expansion of police power to arrest and detain foreigners.² The Pasqua Laws ultimately made it so that individuals formerly classified as legitimate aliens became illegal aliens. The occupation of St. Ambroise (followed by that of the Church of St. Bernard on June 28, 1996) thus gave birth to a new genre of political subjectivity throughout Europe: the *sans papiers*.

At the gathering of the World Social Forum in Porto Alégre, Brazil, in January 2003, the cause of the sans papiers became international when they joined forces with other movements of the dispossessed to help draft "The Statement of the Voiceless," thus forming an international network known as the *no vox*. Frustrated that "the Forum remains a gathering of the "progressive middle classes" that "generates exclusion,"³ and recognizing that political inclusion requires capital, these signatories attempted to create, among other things, a means of financing the attendance of those who could otherwise not afford to participate in the invention and institution of cosmopolitanism.

The political issues surrounding the sans papiers and the no vox are complex and involve debates in international law, citizenship, and human rights more generally. Moreover, as the participants of the St. Ambroise occupation make clear, their status marks an important and heretofore unnoticed distinction between the idea of an "illegal" and one who is not documented—a distinction that further complicates conventional juridical approaches to citizenship. In short, the sans papiers became "illegals" many years after their arrival on European soil, once the ipse dixit of the Pasqua Laws was put into place, declaring immigrant workers without papers illegal immigrants.

By depriving them access to the schema of mimesis, the sans papiers' political status became *anomic*.⁴ Literally lacking a name (because without papers and hence without a fixed signifier), they exist in a mimetic economy that denies them currency. From the perspective of the Pasqua Laws, then, it might seem like the sans papiers' human status is intact (after all, they remain alive). The only real change is a poetic one, some might argue: the change in their legal status is simply a change in signification (from named individual to signifier without a referent). But the point is that the literary recomposition of the legal order alters their status as human subjects as well: Without papers, the sans papiers are suspended from the system of mimetic representation that could afford them their human identity.

The claim I have been making throughout this book is that political accounts of representation are subtly informed and structured by aesthetic modes of representation. Most notably, mimesis—or the ability to accurately portray a reality through an act of representation—is the basis for our understanding of democratic theories of representation. A tacit commitment to a poetics of substitution thus persists in much contemporary political thought. The manner in which we read and write and the theories of literary representation we adopt as our own structure not only our epistemological commitments but also our political thought, thus making for a poetics of political thinking that, in turn, has substantive repercussions for our understandings of the institutional frameworks of legitimate democracies.

There is thus an ethical dimension to how we read and write, to what we read and write for, that informs our moral and political commitments. When engaged in the mimetic mode, our perceptive attentions concentrate on constituencies cast as prediscursively sanctioned because their mode of appearance is easily recognizable within established schemas of representation. With the sans papiers, however, we have an interruption of this circuitry. What was cast as a prediscursively sanctioned form of subjectivity recognizable through an established schema of representation—the legal resident—becomes, through a poetic and juridical act of reconfiguration, incognizable. Now we have the sans papiers, paradoxically a category designed to capture those rendered uncategorizable.

Though it is democratic to represent established constituencies and interests existing within the network of legitimate pluralism, such a drive to mimetic representation is in tension with an equally critical one: a democratic politics of unrepresentability where new modes of action and newly emerging identities—like the sans papiers and the no vox—make the case to creatively pluralize the established registers of justice and legitimacy and find a place on them. The sans papiers' desire to be noticed and counted—to be at once visible and audible—is not easily translatable in mimetic terms. What we are being asked to acknowledge both by the occupations of St. Ambroise and St. Bernard, as well as with the invention of the terms *sans papiers* and *no vox* as signifiers for a new political subjectivity, is the role of unrepresentability as a condition for democratic equality.

The sans papiers are unrecognizable, yet they demand acknowledgment. Lacking a proper name, they are unrepresentable, yet they demand equality. It would be a noble gesture of a beautiful soul to respond to the plight of the sans papiers by giving them papers, by baptizing them with new names and inducting them into the rule of mimesis. Indeed, such a gesture would address one dimension of the sans papiers' claim: repapering would admit inclusion. But there is a secondary problematic at work that insists on the simultaneous importance and inadequacy of mimesis. The paradoxical status of the sans papiers and no vox requires us to rethink our understanding of democratic equality. The emergence of this new form of political subjectivity begs us to question the established partitions that bind the borders not simply of nation-states but of equality itself.

To paraphrase Michel Foucault, the sans papiers and no vox ask that our political thinking "cut off the head of the king."[5] The historical point that accompanies Foucault's charged statement is that the democratic movements of the seventeenth and eighteenth centuries were distinctive in challenging the idea of the proper name.[6] The *citoyen* was someone who had no official title, and hence no proper name. Democratic equality is in this way anomic, standing against the ideal of the proper found in the principle of sovereignty. "If one wants to look for a non-disciplinary form of power," Foucault suggests further, "it is not towards the ancient right of sovereignty that one should turn, but towards the possibility of a new form of right, one which must be anti-disciplinarian, but at the same time liberated from the principle of sovereignty."[7]

What would it mean to think the possibility of "a new form of right"? One way to begin answering such a question might be to think the possibility of a dissensual equality, or disequality, in contrast to the mathematical property of equivalency. Equivalency is a distributive principle allocated by a sovereign authority that operates within an economy of correspondence. Democratic equality, by contrast, implies dissensus. It is the traversing of a logic of correspondence by those whose name is not proper. This is why consensus politics ultimately falters in its appeals to greater and greater inclusion, to more and more representation. To mandate political action thus is ultimately to assume that everyone has the capacity to represent claims in a manner recognizable to those whose reading and writing competencies are already established and well documented. The problem posed by disequality, then, is not simply to endorse the expansion of our domains of distribution. Rather, disequality makes problematic those modes of perception that have preconstituted the scene of political engagement and, in so doing, have determined an a priori order for political participation. In such instances, disequality asks: What forms of intelligibility need to be in place in order to demarcate the limits that exist and govern us now? What modes of action (aural, visual, tactile, etc.) are required in order to disrupt and, indeed, traverse the paradigms of perception enabled by extant governing limits?

Such questions insist on the need to persistently reassess our ideals of representation. While mimesis seems so important in contemporary global settings, it is insufficient to the demands posed by contemporary globalization. Also important but insufficient is our commitment to eliminating contradictions. Democratic politics forces us to confront the tensions that emerge from the disjunctive encounters between dissimilars. In this sense, democratic politics is a politics of the virtual. By virtual I do not mean either unreal or even probable. Democratic politics is virtual because it marks an emergent intensity, a cluster of potentialities whose actualization has not yet been determined but to which we must remain open.[8]

Attending to certain aesthetic features of contemporary political argument alerts us to the way in which an image of political thought carries an ethics of thinking. Moreover, each image contains strategies of appraisal that ensure credence to the value of an idea. Requiring citizens to circumscribe their political thinking to a mode of reasoning akin to a Pauline conversion experience—as we found most forcefully in political liberalism's commitment to satisfying the demands of clarity—is rhetorically effective but also has limits, at least insofar as a goal is to encourage a vibrant and active democracy. Instead, we need also to foster the potential for democratic interruption by acknowledging multiple forms of thinking (whether moral, aesthetic, cultural, cognitive, affective, or otherwise) available to political reflection.

Perhaps, then, the time of democracy arrives when partisans unexpectedly discover the need to respond gracefully to interruption in the hope of creatively accommodating each other, even when no common principle suffices to command the value or shape of such accommodations. To foment the potential of such anomic fissures in the nomenclature of mimesis, we might begin to problematize our own ethic of thinking by asking ourselves what is left out when we model our understandings of political discourse according to the contours of the moral claim? What other modes of claiming are overlooked or marginalized by such a theoretical model? To whom, in short, do we concede the right to think? If it is true that our images of political thought possess a tacit aesthetic component, then it might be worthwhile to pluralize our own poetics of political thinking so that we might be better syntonized with those moments of disequality that might otherwise go unheard.

The point of such problematizations and pluralizations is neither to assert a more accurate mode of political thinking nor to access a conceptually crystalline model of understanding. As shown in the case of the sans papiers, and as Thomas Hobbes warned long ago, emerging political subjectivities will always interrupt our attempts at settling. Thus through the interruptive apertures of disequality political action emerges. Acts of problematization and pluralization engender such apertures availing opportunities of engagement with and instances of resistance to the abundant ambiguities that the world, and life, affords.

Notes

Introduction: Images of Political Thought

1   Arendt, *Lectures on Kant's Political Philosophy*, 21.
2   Deleuze, *Difference and Repetition*, 141.
3   Barthes, "Rhetoric of the Image" in *Image-Music-Text*, 32. Also see Auerbach's discussion of "the figura" as plastic form (from the Latin *fingere*) in his "Figura" in *Scenes from the Drama of European Literatures*, 11–76.
4   Bonnie Honig astutely asks, "In *The Republic*, the founding dialogue of political theory's interminable debate about justice takes place in the house of a foreign merchant, Cephalus, who is originally from Syracuse. Why is this the setting? Does Plato mean to imply that justice, or perhaps philosophical dialogue itself, is occasioned by engagement with foreignness?" (*Democracy and the Foreigner*, 3). My immediate answer to Honig's question is yes. Plato did think that justice and foreignness are intimately related. This is evidenced by the fact that the enlightened individual who returns to the cave to speak to his colleagues is rejected because his experience with brightness transforms him into a foreigner. He comes in from the outside with a field of new experiences that ultimately alienates him from the others.

For a more recent example, consider Cypher (the Judas Iscariot character played by Joe Pantoliano in the 1999 film *The Matrix*), who betrays the members of the Nebuchadnezzar because he wants to be plugged back into the matrix—that is, because he prefers the image world to the real world.

Cypher resents Morpheus and wants to renege on his initial choice—the choice of the red pill over the blue pill—because, like Plato's individual, he realizes that having been dragged out of the matrix, he has become a foreigner, an alien in a world where he cannot belong. This is why, in the crucial scene where he is at dinner eating the steak with the agents, Cypher wants to be assured that all his memories of the real world will be erased.

5 Plato, *The Republic*, 210.

6 Frye, *Anatomy of Criticism*, 14.

7 In this regard, I am indebted to a series of contemporary thinkers whose work on politics and aesthetics is influential to my thinking, including, but certainly not limited to, Amanda Anderson, F. R. Ankersmit, Jane Bennett, Judith Butler, Stanley Cavell, Bill Connolly, Frances Ferguson, Stanley Fish, Richard Flathman, Michael Fried, John Guillory, Bonnie Honig, Steven Knapp, Kirstie McClure, Anne Norton, Martha Nussbaum (despite my criticism of her in the subsequent section), Jacques Rancière, and Mort Schoolman.

8 Larmore, *The Morals of Modernity*, 192.

9 On this general assumption, see Jane Bennett's account, discussion, and critique of "The Dangers of Aestheticization" in *The Enchantment of Modern Life*, 148–52.

10 Böhrer, *Suddenness*. See also "The Aesthetics of Fear," in Fisher, *The Vehement Passions*, 132–56.

11 The number of authors who argue against the "aestheticization of politics" and link aesthetics to Weimar Germany is too many to list. Worthy of mention, however, are Richard Wolin's *The Terms of Cultural Criticism*, Jürgen Habermas's *The Philosophical Discourse of Modernity*, and Peter Cohen's film *The Architecture of Doom*. Of course, these modern examples are only the most recent chapter in a long history of distrust toward the theater, the arts, and symbolic representation more generally, and literary circles are not immune from such anxieties. In the nineteenth century, the *l'art pour l'art* movement as imagined by Flaubert and Baudelaire pursued a commitment to a pure form of art immune from social and political concerns. I discuss elements of l'art pour l'art in chapter 3. For a more sustained discussion, see Pierre Bourdieu's "The Conquest of Autonomy," in *The Rules of Art*, and Frances Ferguson's "Emma, or Happiness (or Sex Work)."

12 There are, of course, other figurations of the poetic than the one adopted here. I am thinking of Martin Heidegger's attempts, later in life, to account for the status of the work of art (see "The Origin of the Work of Art," in *Poetry, Language, Thought*) or Hans-Georg Gadamer's herme-

neutics (*Truth and Method*). Though I appreciate both Heidegger's and Gadamer's insights, my resistance to adopting either of these approaches rests in the fact that both thinkers—in different though parallel ways—retain the strong Kantian commitment to distinguishing between aesthetic and moral evaluation. This is not to say, of course, that a politics could not be surmised from their efforts, nor that their insights are not ethically relevant. It is to say, however, that there is a resistance on both their parts to attend to the relationship between aesthetic and political thinking. Most notably with Heidegger, for instance, his commitment to the estrangement of the work of art treats aesthetic experience as a state of exception that radically alienates the work of art. As George Bruns states, "The radical otherness [of the work of art] means that we can make no place for it within any framework that makes the world an intelligible object for us" (*Heidegger's Estrangements*, 45) In adopting such a perspective, Heidegger refuses the productivity of the work of art; art is, in its nature, poetic to the extent that it possesses the power of "un-becoming." In this radical hermeneutics of aesthetic experience, then, Heidegger wants the work of art to do the work of defamiliarization but not for the sake of either subjectivity or self-consciousness. That is, it is not an experience of otherness that the work of art provides. Instead, it is an ontological rift between consciousness and being. My concern is that such a radical rift is, in principle, apolitical because of its refusal of engaging the role of subjectivity in aesthetic experience. Or, to put the matter slightly differently, it seems that Heidegger's concern with the aesthetic object refuses an engagement with the social work of judgment in aesthetic evaluation.

13   Poison, "Every Rose Has Its Thorn."

14   Ricoeur, *The Rule of Metaphor*. The unfortunate mistranslation of Ricoeur's "la métaphore vive" into "the rule of metaphor" does much to undo Ricoeur's defense of an interactive theory of metaphor, as his discussion has little to do with either a procedural account of metaphor or its sovereignty—as the term *rule* might imply.

15   Ricoeur, "Metaphor and the Central Problem of Hermeneutics," in *Hermeneutics and the Human Sciences*, 174.

16   Arendt, *The Human Condition*, 178.

17   Ricoeur imposes limits on his own adoption of the interactive view of metaphor that I engage in "The Predicative Function in Ideology."

18   Walter Benn Michaels's critique of cultural difference is relevant and punctual. In *Our America*, "Political Science Fictions," and *The Shape of the Signifier*, Michaels presents a robust critique of antiessentialist theories of difference. His main point is that antiessentialist critiques of identity

politics rely on an inherent essentialism that posits difference as an innate quality of culture. Michaels's argument is convincing, however, only if you rely on the idea that difference (or diversity) is a quality that an object can possess, just like "blackness" or "Americanness." What Michaels himself overlooks, along with the antiessentialist theorists he criticizes, is the possibility that difference is not a property of an object but a force in the world.

19 Yunis, *Taming Democracy*, 141. The passage from Euripides reads as follows: "Thou givest me here an advantage, as it might be in a game of draughts; for the city, whence I come, is ruled by one man only, not by the mob; none there puffs up the citizens with specious words, and for his own advantage twists them this way or that, one moment dear to them and lavish of his favours, the next a bane to all; and yet by fresh calumnies of others he hides his former failures and escapes punishment. *Besides, how shall the people, if it cannot form true judgments, be able rightly to direct the state?* Nay, 'tis time, not haste, that affords a better understanding. A poor hind, granted be he not all unschooled, would still be unable from his toil to give his mind to politics. Verily the better sort count it no healthy sign when the worthless man obtains a reputation by beguiling with words the populace, though aforetime he was naught" (emphasis added).

20 On theatrocracy, see Rancière's discussion of Plato's treatment of public spectacles and the "barbaric" practice of applauding: "The noise of number—the very custom of applauding, imported from Italy—is what has created theatrocracy. Power is not so much in the spectacle itself as in the racket that it authorizes" (*The Philosopher and His Poor*, 47).

21 On the public display of value, see Frances Ferguson's *Pornography, the Theory*, especially her critical reading of Foucault's treatment of Bentham's social innovations (17–25). For Ferguson, "Bentham's answer to the problem of the monopolization of societal recognition was to imagine that the new disciplinary social structures would regularly be devised to capture previously imperceptible kinds of action and to discern their value. Value was everywhere—but latently. Panoptic structures made value explicit and in that sense gave it perceptible weight" (24).

22 Honig, *Democracy and the Foreigner*, 112.

23 Nussbaum, "The Professor of Parody," 38.

24 See Thomas and Turner, *Clear and Simple as the Truth*. For a historical example, see Jonathan Rée's discussion of Ralphe Lever's *The Arte of Reason, rightly termed, Witcraft, teaching a perfect way to argue and dispute* (London, 1573) in "The Translation of Philosophy." Finally, Michael Warner's discussion of the Nussbaum's polemic in *Publics and Counterpublics* (125–58) is also noteworthy.

25 Nussbaum, *Love's Knowledge*, 3.

26 Nussbaum's implicit charge of obscurity assumes that terms like *reflective equilibrium*, *deontology*, or *normativity* belong to a non-jargon-laden, "common" discourse. The problem of obscurity, however, may be something that the discipline of philosophy cannot do without. As Jonathan Rée has noted, "in philosophy, alone amongst the theoretical disciplines, obscurity may be precisely the quality that makes a work a classic; it indicates not that the text happens to be inadequately worked out, but that it is a sensitive and artfully elaborated documentation of an essentially intractable enigma, an exemplary embodiment of the bafflement in which philosophy takes its rise" ("The Translation of Philosophy," 227).

27 Nussbaum, *Love's Knowledge*, 141–42.

28 Nussbaum, *Poetic Justice*, 45–46.

29 That Nussbaum also chooses Derrida as an example of someone who is inadequately attuned to ethical matters is simply astounding, given Derrida's philosophical commitments to an ethics of reading and writing, especially in *Of Grammatology*, *Writing and Difference*, and *Margins of Philosophy*.

30 Nussbaum, *Poetic Justice*, 36.

31 For a similar critique, see Michael Warner's excellent discussion of counterpublics and "the ideology of reading" in *Publics and Counterpublics*, 123.

32 Hume, "Of the Standard of Taste," in *Essays*, 244.

33 Hunter, "Aesthetics and Cultural Studies," in *Cultural Studies*, 353.

34 Deleuze, "Literature and Life," in *Essays*, 1.

35 Foucault, "A Preface to Transgression," in *Language, Counter-Memory, Practice*, 34.

36 On the ethics of a "fusion of horizons" in hermeneutic experience, see Hans-Georg Gadamer's *Truth and Method*. On the relationship between narrativity, ethics, and alterity, see Paul Ricoeur's discussion of three-fold mimesis in *Time and Narrative*, especially his discussion of mimesis, 1:76–82.

37 Deleuze, *Difference and Repetition*, 64.

Chapter 1: Hobbes's Science of Politics

1 Blair, "Annotating and Indexing Natural Philosophy," 2.

2 Janet Lyon makes a similar point when, discussing the manifesto, she asserts that "the public performance of 'we' in polemical tracts provided

an edge of urgency that was sharply at odds with the gradualist agenda of political modernity" (*Manifestoes*, 11).

3   See for instance, Alan Bloom's *The Closing of the American Mind*.

4   Rancière, *The Names of History*, 30.

5   I take this to be the point of Jürgen Habermas's discussion of Samuel Richardson's *Pamela* and the rise of the bourgeois public sphere in *The Structural Transformation of the Public Sphere*. Referring explicitly to Richardson's invention of the psychological novel, he states that "the relations between author, work, and public changed. They became intimate mutual relationships between privatized individuals who were psychologically interested in what was 'human' in self-knowledge, and in empathy" (50). See my discussion of Habermas in chapter 4.

6   Hobbes, *Leviathan*, 10. As a possible interlocutor with Hobbes, consider Abeizer Coppe's cover page to *A Fiery Flying Roll*, stating that the text was "Imprinted at *London*, in the beginning of that notable day, wherein the secret of all hearts are laid open; and wherein the worst and foulest of villanies, are discovered under the best and fairest outsides" (*Selected Writings*, 15).

7   The *Oxford English Dictionary* defines *oracle* as an utterance of deep import or wisdom; an opinion or declaration regarded as authoritative and infallible; undeniable truth.

8   I would like to thank Richard Tuck for helping me formulate this question.

9   See Sheldon Wolin's classic formulation in *Politics and Vision*, 248–57.

10 I am not interested in looking at nominalism as a theophilosophical position, but I am interested in Hobbes's rhetorical use of nominalism as a device for aggregating opinion. As a device or instrument of representation, nominalism is no different than an opinion poll.

11 Shklar, "The Liberalism of Fear," 24.

12 Berlin, *Four Essays on Liberty*, 126.

13 Here I would cite Hobbes's empiricism, and more specifically, his notion that there are forces in the world and that our knowledge depends on the impact of things upon our senses as a source for what I am suggesting is a more nuanced and, indeed, horizontal metaphysics of power.

14 Tracy B. Strong makes a similar claim in his essay "How to Write Scripture: Words, Authority, and Politics in Thomas Hobbes." Strong argues that Hobbes relies on divine creation, drawing on an understanding of scripture developed through Lutheran Protestantism and the Reformation more generally. Though sympathetic to Strong's claims, my argument deemphasizes the authoritarian features of *Leviathan* and focuses on the

twin aesthetico-political function of representation in Hobbes's thought and writings.

15 See Hobbes's discussion of poetics in his reply to Sir William Davenant's preface to "A Discourse upon *Gondibert*" in *The Later Renaissance in England*. On this point, see also Quentin Skinner's *Reason and Rhetoric in the Philosophy of Hobbes*.

16 Pitkin, *The Concept of Representation*, 15.
17 Oakeshott, *Rationalism in Politics*, 232.
18 Johnston, *The Rhetoric of Leviathan*, 23.
19 I take this to be the thrust of Wolin's reading in *Politics and Vision*.
20 Skinner, *Reason and Rhetoric in the Philosophy of Hobbes*, 363.
21 Skinner breaks Hobbes down into three periodicities: his early humanist writings, his middle "scientific" works where he "rejects" eloquence, and his later return to *ornatus* that culminates in *Leviathan*.
22 John Rowlands explains that "de Dinteville's presence in England was connected with the French negotiations at the Vatican conducted by de Dinteville's brother, François, the Bishop of Auxerre, whereby Francis I's second son, the Duke of Orleans, was to be betrothed to the Pope's niece." The English were given to understand that in return for approving this union, the papacy would not condemn Henry's marriage to Anne. "However, the Papacy was not accommodating and instead secretly recognized the French claim to Milan, while France agreed, in return, to undertake a strong anti-reformist policy" (*Holbein*, 85–86).
23 Rawls, *Political Liberalism*, xxiv.
24 I rely on Jurgis Baltrusaitis's account of the painting in his *Anamorphic Art*, 91–114.
25 Baltrusaitis, *Anamorphic Art*, 96.
26 Ibid., 98.
27 Ibid., 104.
28 Ibid., 104–5.
29 In what is perhaps the key section of *The Sublime Object of Ideology*, Slavoj Žižek states that we could denote the "properly ideological perspective" as an "error of perspective," and further, "we could denote this 'error of perspective' as ideological anamorphosis. Lacan often refers to Holbein's 'Ambassadors': if we look at what appears from the frontal view as an extended, 'erected' meaningless spot, from the right perspective we notice the contours of a skull. The criticism of ideology must perform a somewhat homologous operation: if we look at the element which holds together the ideological edifice, at this 'phallic,' erected Guarantee of Meaning, from the right (or, more precisely—politically speaking—left)

perspective, we are able to recognize in it the embodiment of a lack, of a chasm of non-sense gaping in the midst of ideological meaning" (99–100).

30 Greenblatt, *Renaissance Self-Fashioning*, 21. Greenblatt's account is worth quoting at length: "Holbein fuses a radical questioning of the status of the world with a radical questioning of the status of art. For the painting insists, passionately and profoundly, on the representational power of art, its central role in man's apprehension and control of reality, even as it insists, with uncanny persuasiveness, on the fictional character of that entire so-called reality and the art that pretends to represent it. In the context of our normal relationship to a painting—indeed in the context of the physical stance we conventionally assume before any object we have chosen to perceive—the marginal position is an eccentric flight of fancy, virtually a non-place, just as the skull exists in a non-place in relation to all the other objects Holbein depicts."

31 In *The Curious Perspective*, Ernest Gilman notes that the anamorphic skull is also a clever signature, as the word *holbein* literally means "hollow bone."

32 Tuck, *Philosophy and Government*, 286. As a side note, this chapter was written before the publication of Noel Malcolm's outstanding historical study on Hobbes and *anamorphosis* (*Aspects of Hobbes*). For a detailed account of Hobbes's fascination with anamorphic devices and, indeed, with perspectivism more generally, Malcolm's study is invaluable.

33 Baltrusaitis, *Anamorphic Art*, 111.

34 Tuck, *Philosophy and Government*, 287.

35 Hobbes, *Leviathan*, part 1, chap. 15, 110.

36 Ibid.

37 The conclusion to Hobbes's *A Minute or First Draught of the Optiques* ends: "I shall deserve the reputation of having been ye first to lay ye ground of two sciences, this of optiques, ye most curious, and ye other of natural justice, which i have done in my book *de Cive*, ye most profitable of all other" (quoted in Caygill, *The Art of Judgment*, 19).

38 Thucydides, *The Peloponnesian War*, xxiii.

39 Ibid.

40 Ibid., emphasis added.

41 The first line reads: "For this last half year I have been troubled with the disease (as I may call it) of translation; the cold prose fits of it, which are always the most tedious with me, were spent in the History of the League: the hot, which succeeded them, in this volume of Verse Miscellanies." Dryden, "Sylvae: or, the Second Part of Poetical Miscellanies," in *Essays of John Dryden*, 251.

NOTES TO CHAPTER 1   133

42   Flathman, "Book Review of Skinner's *Reason and Rhetoric in the Philosophy of Hobbes*," 821.

43   Hobbes, *Leviathan*, 10.

44   Skinner, "Hobbes and the Purely Artificial Person of the State." See especially 4n18.

45   Tuck, *Philosophy and Government*, 327.

46   Corbett and Lightbown, *The Comely Frontispiece*, 222.

47   Ibid., 230.

48   There is a drawn title page (1651) that has cherubic faces that comprise the body of the Leviathan and look out at the observer, but this was not used as the original frontispiece.

49   Caygill, *The Art of Judgment*, 25.

50   Ibid., 24.

51   Hobbes, *Leviathan*, part 1, chap. 8, 50–51.

52   It is worth remarking that in his estimation of discernment over wit, Hobbes is distancing himself from an Aristotelian, scholastic tradition of rhetoric that privileges the ability to form similitudes over all other intellectual activities: "But the greatest thing by far," Aristotle asserts in his *Poetics*, "is to be master of metaphor. It is the one thing that cannot be learnt from others; and it is also a sign of genius, since a good metaphor implies an intuitive perception of the similarity in dissimilars" (Aristotle, *Poetics*, 1459 a5–8, in *The Complete Works of Aristotle*). Hobbes reverses this binary by privileging the ability to determine differences over similarities.

53   Hobbes, "To the Readers," xxi.

54   For further consideration see Kevin Sharpe's essay "An Image Dotting Rabble," in Sharpe and Zwicker, *Refiguring Revolutions*.

55   Hobbes, *Leviathan*, part 1, chap. 16, 112.

56   See the *Oxford English Dictionary*, 2nd ed., s.v. *hypocrite*.

57   See Hobbes's use of the term *mark* in *Leviathan*, part 1, chap. 4.

58   Hobbes, *Leviathan*, part 2, chap. 21, 145.

59   I borrow this formulation from Stephen Greenblatt's discussion of Holbein's *Ambassadors* in *Renaissance Self-Fashioning*, 23.

60   Hobbes, *Leviathan*, part 2, chap. 21, 145.

61   As occurs most vividly when electors choose not to reelect an incumbent for whom they had previously voted.

62   My reading contrasts with Sheldon Wolin's attempt at linking Hobbes's "science of politics" to geometry: "If the role of definitions in political philosophy was to supply the fundamental rules underpinning society," Wolin concludes, "these definitions must be based upon a form of knowledge as certain and immutable as the truths of geometry" (*Politics*

and Vision, 254). As we have seen, for Hobbes geometry and perspectivism coincide, thereby denying the possibility of immutable truths.

63 Hobbes, *Leviathan*, part 1, chap. 7, 47. I would stress here the resonances with an Erasmian critique of the vanity of knowledge—a resonance that persists throughout Hobbes's oeuvre.

64 Hobbes, *Leviathan*, part I, chap. 7, 48.

65 In other words, Hobbes is not a participant in what Michel Foucault calls "the modern episteme" (*The Order of Things*, part 2).

66 Hobbes, *Leviathan*, 483.

67 Hobbes, "To the Readers," xxi.

68 Hobbes, *Leviathan*, part 2, chap. 21, 145.

Chapter 2: Deleuze's Ethics of the Problem

1 Deleuze, *Difference and Repetition*, 51.

2 Ibid., 50.

3 In their discussion of wonder and the monstrous, Daston and Park make a similar claim: "In the works of the learned, the vulgar stood as the antonym of enlightenment; they were barbarous, ignorant, and unruly. When, in the early eighteenth century, the "love of the marvelous" also came to be seen as the hallmark of the vulgar, it was a sure sign that the enlightenment and the marvelous were no longer compatible" (*Wonders and the Order of Nature*, 343).

4 Bakhtin, *Rabelais and His World*, 50.

5 Montaigne, "That to Philosophize Is to Learn to Die," in *The Complete Essays*, 65.

6 See Colie, *Paradoxia Epidemica* (231–33).

7 Bakhtin, *Rabelais and His World*, 23.

8 We need not turn to the great thinkers of the early modern period for an illustration of this; there are also examples from more mundane figures of the period. Consider, in this regard, the sixteenth-century miller Menocchio from Montereale. As Carlo Ginzburg has documented, this contemporary of Montaigne's spent most of his life constructing a fragmented and paradoxical, though fantastic, cosmology that threatened church officials to such a degree that he was placed under the Inquisition and forced to recant his views. "With an unselfconscious and open mind," Ginzburg explains, Menocchio "made use of remnants of the thinking of others as he might stones and bricks. But the linguistic and conceptual tools that he tried to acquire were neither neutral nor innocent. This is the ex-

planation for most of the contradictions, uncertainties, and incongruities of his speeches. Using terms infused with Christianity, neo-Platonism, and scholastic philosophy, Menocchio tried to express the elemental, instinctive materialism of generation after generation of peasants" (*The Cheese and the Worms*, 61).

9   Quine, "Paradox," 92.
10 Colie, *Paradoxia Epidemica*, 3.
11 In his introduction to the Rabelais book, Bakhtin refers to L. E. Pinsky's claim that "the grotesque in art is related to the paradox in logic. At first glance, the grotesque is merely witty and amusing, but it contains great potentialities" (32n12).
12 Colie, *Paradoxia Epidemica*, 10.
13 Richard McKeon states that "the relevance of the methods of rhetoric to the problems of philosophy is due in part to the continuity of the influences in which the methods of philosophy have influenced the methods of rhetoric and been influenced in turn by them" (*Rhetoric*, 64).
14 Fish, *Surprised by Sin*, 22.
15 In another essay, "Rhetoric," Fish explains further that the line "defects of our hearers" first appears in Aristotle's *Rhetoric* (3.1404.8) and that it would have been recognizable as such by Milton's readers (*Doing What Comes Naturally*, 476).
16 For a discussion of the characterology of argument, see Amanda Anderson's "Pragmatism and Character."
17 Fish, *Surprised by Sin*, 6.
18 Richard McKeon argues that there was a development and displacement of dialectics from rhetoric to logic in the early modern period. McKeon explains that "during the 12th century logic was distinguished from dialectic; and rhetoric became a counterpart of dialectic, although logic continued to be divided into judgment and discovery.... The effects of this extension of the devices of rhetoric to logic became apparent, in turn, in the treatment of rhetoric, and it became important to contrast rhetoric and dialectic when both rhetoricians and dialecticians made use of 'places' for purposes of discovery" (*Rhetoric*, 134).
19 Fish, *Surprised by Sin*, 7.
20 Shuger, *Sacred Rhetoric*, 9.
21 Ibid., 138.
22 Participation also falls under the schema of the aesthetico-philosophic triplet, such that the triad of the forms participation is material-imitative-demonic. See Deleuze, *Expressionism in Philosophy*, 169.
23 The language of artifact is implied in Deleuze and Guattari's ac-

count of philosophy as "the art of forming, inventing, and fabricating concepts" (*What Is Philosophy?*, 2).

24 Deleuze, *The Logic of Sense*, 256.

25 Ibid., 257.

26 Ibid.

27 Deleuze, *Difference and Repetition*, 127. In this sense, Deleuze's criticism of Plato differs from Jacques Derrida's project of the deconstruction of Western metaphysics. Whereas Derrida focuses on the master-subject relation implied in the Model/copy binary, Deleuze sees this binary as precisely that which allows for Platonism to subsist. Unlike Derrida, Deleuze is interested less in deconstructing Plato's metaphysical binaries than he is in showing the extent to which Platonism is premised on a series of moral prerequisites to thinking and demonstrating that these prerequisites have explicit ethical and political ramifications for a procedure of selection.

28 I discuss the distinction between the sym-bolic and the dia-bolic in "The Predicative Function in Ideology."

29 Deleuze, *Difference and Repetition*, 59–60.

30 Ibid., 61.

31 Ibid., 63.

32 It would be a mistake to respond to Deleuze's observations, as some do, with an appeal to discourse ethics, since the issue of demonic participation exposes the inadequacy of a pragmatics of communication for political participation. Whereas a Habermasian model of communicative action, for instance, might insist on the correction of one's speech acts so as to maximize inclusion within the formal structure of communication, the problem raised by the aesthetico-philosophic triplet questions precisely that impetus to correct utterances so as to make them recognizable. The false claimants are not excluded in discussion to the extent that they are recognized as "false claimants." Thus, an appeal to greater inclusiveness through "better speech" is insufficient. Rather, the force of Deleuze's critique is to show that by occupying the position of demonic participation, the false claimant cannot be recognized as "one who claims."

33 Jacques Derrida's most sustained treatment of Plato is in his *Dissemination*.

34 Deleuze, *Difference and Repetition*, 62.

35 On the "un-quiet" of the demos, see Arendt's discussion of the *vita activa* in *The Human Condition*, 12–17.

36 Deleuze, *The Logic of Sense*, 262.

37 Deleuze, *Difference and Repetition*, 127.

38 Rotman, *Signifying Nothing*, 59.

39 Kaplan, *The Nothing That Is*, 110.

40 The term *risk*, also Arabic in origin, translates as "earning one's daily bread," suggesting that, at least in Mediterranean culture, investment risk is a legitimate form of earning (Drucker, *The Practice of Management*, 46).

41 Camille, *Master of Death*, 15. This anxiety does not dissipate and, as Shapin and Schaffer point out in *Leviathan and the Air-Pump*, can also be found in Hobbes's debates with Boyle.

42 Camille, *Master of Death*, 16.

43 In *Confessions* (book 7) Augustine discusses the spatial and temporal dimensions of God. "Whatever had no dimension in space," he concludes, "must be absolutely nothing at all. If it did not or could not have qualities at all, it must be absolutely nothing at all" (111). Further, "if things are deprived of all good, they cease altogether to be; and this means that as long as they are, they are good. Therefore, whatever is, is good; and evil, the origin of which I was trying to find, is not a substance, because if it were a substance, it would be good" (125).

44 Duns Scotus, *Duns Scotus Metaphysician*, 109. This particular passage is taken from the *Opus oxoniense*.

45 Alain Badiou, *Deleuze*, 39. The translation is my own. The French passage reads, "L'univocité ne signifie pas d'abord que l'être soit numériquement un, ce qui est une assertion vide. L'Un n'est pas ici celui du compte ou de l'identité, et la pensée a déjà renoncé si elle imagine qu'il y a un seul et même Etre. . . . L'univocité n'est pas non plus que la pensée soit tautologique (l'Un est l'Un). Elle est pleinement compatible avec l'existence de multiples formes de l'Etre."

46 Pearson, *Germinal Life*, 15.

47 Deleuze, *Difference and Repetition*, 35. Importantly, Deleuze's last paragraph in *Difference and Repetition* is also a discussion of the univocity of Being, thus suggesting that this concept, at least in layout if not in fact, frames the entire discussion: "The univocity of being and individuating difference are connected outside representation as profoundly as generic difference and specific difference are connected within representation from the point of view of analogy. Univocity signifies that being itself is univocal, while that of which it is said is equivocal: precisely the opposite of analogy" (304).

48 Deleuze, *The Logic of Sense*, 179–80.

49 Quoted in Deleuze, *Difference and Repetition*, 44.

50 Colletti, *Marxism and Hegel*, 18.

51 Deleuze, *Difference and Repetition*, 131.

52 Ibid., 129.

53 Ibid., 131.

54 Ibid.

55 This is the critical purchase of Deleuze's grammatical distinction—found throughout his writings—between the noun *thought* and gerund *thinking*. Deleuze wants the gerund to do the kind of work of becoming that the noun (committed, as all nouns are, to a logic of identity) cannot.

56 Deleuze, *Difference and Repetition*, 139.

57 Deleuze, *The Logic of Sense*, 74 and 77.

58 Deleuze, *Difference and Repetition*, 141. This points to a further similarity between Deleuze and Nietzsche. Consider this passage from *The Will to Power*: "The subjective compulsion not to contradict here is a biological compulsion: the instinct for the utility of inferring as we do is part of us, we almost are this instinct—But what naïveté to extract from this the proof that we are therewith in possession of a 'truth in itself'!—Not being able to contradict is proof of an incapacity, not of 'truth'" (sec. 521).

59 "Avatars of the Tortoise" is Jorge Luis Borges's expression for thinkers who are taken by paradox as a mode of thinking (see *Labyrinths*, 202–9). With respect to paradox, it is worth noting a profound connection between Deleuze's critique of "difference as negation" and Theodore Adorno's aesthetic theory. Specifically, both thinkers exhibit an appreciation for what Mort Schoolman calls "aesthetic individuality" (see his *Reason and Horror*, especially chapter 6, "An Ethic of Appearances"). In the case of Adorno, as Schoolman points out, this is most evident in his desire to recast the art object as an object of ethical experience, so as to "sustain a notion of aesthetic rationality, which through the art work, encourages a sensibility to the harm inflicted on difference in every attempt to cross the divide and make the unknown known as though the world conformed to its representations" (149).

Though Deleuze would probably resist the language of an "aesthetic rationality" as too cognitive and not sufficiently somatic in its ascriptions, there is in both thinkers a Nietzschean commitment to paradox that challenges the possibility (and indeed, ethical sustainability) of treating difference mimetically, as a quality that one can ascribe to things (see my discussion of Adorno and essay writing in chapter 4). Thus, what each thinker develops through their aesthetic insights is an appreciation of the profundity of surfaces that entails a rethinking of "difference" as merely negation. (Also relevant is Nikolas Kompridis's discussion of an ideal of receptivity in Adorno's theory of music in "Amidst the Plurality of Voices.")

60 Deleuze, *Difference and Repetition*, 145. In the chapter previous to

the one I am quoting from, Deleuze explains that the "dark precursor" is the name given to the force that allows for communication between divergent series to take place. The demonic allusions here are not to be overlooked as this "Satanic rhetoric" persists throughout Deleuze's discussion: "Thunderbolts explode between different intensities, but they are preceded by an invisible *dark precursor*, which determines their path in advance but in reverse, as though intagliated" (119).

61 Deleuze, *Difference and Repetition*, 204.
62 Ibid., 64.
63 Ibid., 35. Also see Deleuze's "To Have Done with Judgment," in *Essays*, 126–35.
64 Deleuze, *The Logic of Sense*, 71.
65 Foucault, *The History of Sexuality*, 88–89: "In political thought and analysis," Foucault asserts, "we still have not cut off the head of the king."
66 Deleuze, *Difference and Repetition*, 64.

Chapter 3: Rawls and Rancière

1 Cicero, *De Oratore* III, 195.
2 Habermas, "The Rawls/Habermas Exchange," 109.
3 See McClure, *The Odor of Judgment*. McClure correlates Arendt's "thinking in company with others" with Mikhail Bakhtin's account of dialogic responsiveness: "Arendt's thinking in company, in this respect, is a thinking-in-response—in Bakhtin's terms an 'answer-word' to another's utterance that is itself, as a public utterance, directed to the 'answer-words' of still others—that differs quite radically from the complacency that typically inhabits the notion of 'conversation,'" 59.
4 Arendt, "The Crisis in Culture," in *Between Past and Future*, 174.
5 As a word of caution, I want to specify at the outset that my analysis is not concerned exclusively with the content of what each thinker values (that is, the "what" of value). Rather, I focus on the function of value in the role of argumentation, asking how concerns about the status of value structure each thinker's observations about justice.
6 Guillory, *Cultural Capital*, 303.
7 Gilles Deleuze explains that "in aesthetic judgment the reflected representation of the form causes the higher pleasure of the beautiful. We must then recognize that the higher state of the faculty of feeling has two paradoxical characteristics which are intimately linked. On the one hand, contrary to what happens in the case of the other faculties, the higher form

here does not define any interest in reason: aesthetic pleasure is independent both of speculative interest and of the practical interest and, indeed, is itself defined as completely disinterested. On the other hand, the faculty of feeling in its higher form is not legislative: all legislation implies objects on which it is exercised and which are subject to it" (*Kant's Critical Philosophy*, 47).

8   Kant, *Critique of Judgment*, 51.

9   Kant states that "we call *agreeable* what GRATIFIES us, *beautiful* what we just LIKE, *good* what we ESTEEM, or *endorse* [*billigen*], i.e., that to which we attribute [*setzen*] an objective value . . . We may say that, of all these three kinds of liking, only the liking involved in taste for the beautiful is disinterested and *free*, since we are not compelled to give our approval by any interest, whether of sense or of reason" (*Critique of Judgment*, 52). It is worth specifying that "the good" that involves "a pure practical liking" is not the same as "a good"—an end toward which individuals direct themselves. Rather, "the good" is equivalent to Kant's idea of "the right," and willing the good is a sign of virtue.

10   Ferguson, *Solitude and the Sublime*, 7 (emphasis added). See also J. F. Lyotard's discussion on the relationship between aesthetics and ethics in the third critique in his *Lessons on the Analytic of the Sublime*, 159-90.

11   More simply put, Kant's argument is that we can all agree that an aesthetic object is an object of value (i.e., beautiful), whether we like it or not.

12   Kant, *Critique of Judgment*, 59.

13   Ibid.

14   See Arendt's discussion of the public realm, the common, and the *inter homines esse* in *The Human Condition*, 50-58.

15   Ferguson, *Solitude and the Sublime*, 5.

16   In another relevant passage, Kant repeats his claim that "the pleasure we take in the beautiful is a pleasure neither of enjoyment, nor of a law-governed activity, nor yet of a reasoning contemplation governed by ideas, but is a pleasure of mere reflection" (ibid., 158).

17   Ibid., 160.

18   A similar instance is Rousseau's famous account of the first fence in history in his *Discourse on Inequality*. The effect of that first boundary is not only to delineate ownership of property, but also to allow individuals to compare their selves with the selves of others.

19   Recall the first lines of Kant's *An Answer to the Question: "What is Enlightenment?"* in *Kant's Political Writings*: "Enlightenment," he asserts, "is man's emergence from his self-incurred tutelage. Tutelage is the in-

ability to use one's own understanding without the guidance of another." Accountability is the means by which we can free ourselves from the guidance or tutelage of others. The ability to justify our own judgments means that we do not have to rely on any form of authority other than our own, and in this respect, we become free.

20 As far as I know, no moral theorist to date has justified why it is that moral arguments should be read exclusively for their epistemic content and not for their formal aesthetic qualities, literary or otherwise.

21 Fried, *Art and Objecthood*, 151.

22 Rawls, *Collected Papers*, 585.

23 Ibid., 478.

24 Ibid., 614. This is also the manner in which Rawls distinguishes his project from Jürgen Habermas's project of communicative action and a discourse theory of ethics. For an elaboration of this point, see the Rawls/Habermas exchange.

25 See Rawls's "Justice as Fairness: Political not Metaphysical," in *Collected Papers*. See also Sheldon Wolin's review of *Political Liberalism*, "The Liberal-Democratic Divide."

26 Rawls, *Collected Papers*, 580.

27 Rawls, *Political Liberalism*, 218.

28 See Saul Kripke's discussion of "primal baptism" in his *Naming and Necessity*.

29 Rawls, *Collected Papers*, 585.

30 Ibid.

31 Ibid., 586.

32 On this distinction, see Rawls's discussion of "nonpublic reason" in *Political Liberalism*, 220.

33 To be sure, consensus on the possibility of nonrhetorical argument is far from secure, as the plethora of publications from Stanley Fish's pen evince (see especially his *Doing What Comes Naturally* and *The Trouble with Principle*).

34 Arendt, *Between Past and Future*, 262.

35 Whether the integrity of such a totality is at all sustainable is a matter that has received a substantial amount of attention (and press) in literary criticism, especially since the arrival of Derridean deconstruction onto North American shores in the 1960s (see Macksey and Donato, *The Structuralist Controversy*).

36 My discussion of narrative is entirely indebted to Paul Ricoeur's monumental *Time and Narrative*, especially volume 1.

37 Jonathan Rée, "The Translation of Philosophy," 228. The problem

of "voice" in theoretical literacy, Rée explains, is most explicit when translating verb tenses and temporal styles. Something like indirect speech, for instance, might be conditional in French, subjunctive in German, and past imperfect in English. Though these difficulties are discussed in reference to translating "conversational storytelling," Rée shows how these problems are not limited to literary works, but are problems of language that make themselves most felt when tackling the dilemmas surrounding translation; dilemmas, I submit, that were exceedingly apparent to thinkers like Thomas Hobbes, for instance (see chapter 1).

38 Ricoeur, *Time and Narrative*, 1:70–73. Here more than ever Ricoeur shows his indebtedness to Gadamer.

39 Cornell, *Defending Ideals*, 44. Further into the essay Cornell touches on the possibility of a Rawlsian aesthetic when she discusses the place of "conjectural reasoning" as a duty of civility in Rawls's later writings, and especially in "The Idea of Public Reason Revisited." She explains that Rawls's reformulation of public reason asks us — in her words — to "imagine that someone who may seem very strange to us is reasonable and rational and that the experience of strangeness must not be translated into a judgment of inferiority" (54).

40 Rawls, *Political Liberalism*, 237. Judith Shklar, who in her "Liberalism of Fear" essay also marks the religious wars as the historical origins of political liberalism, shares a similar sentiment regarding the stature of the judicial system: "The paradigm of politics is the tribunal in which fair rules and decisions are made to satisfy the greatest possible number of demands made by individual citizens against one another individually, and against the government and other socially powerful institutions" (26).

41 Hume, *An Enquiry Concerning the Principles of Morals*, section 3, *Of Justice*. Also see Rawls's *Lectures on the History of Moral Philosophy*, "Hume III — Justice as an Artificial Virtue."

42 Rawls, *Political Liberalism*, 239–40.

43 I use the language of "acknowledgment" rather than "recognition" because I have been convinced of its value as a political project by Patchen Markell's excellent study and critique of the politics of recognition, *Bound by Recognition*.

44 This also explains the exemplarity of the space wherein Supreme Court decisions are made.

45 Rawls, "Justice as Fairness," in *Collected Papers*.

46 See Bourdieu's "The Conquest of Autonomy," in *The Rules of Art*. Extending Bourdieu's discussion, Frances Ferguson's "Emma, or Happiness (or Sex Work)" examines Flaubert's trial and subsequent defense

strategy revolving around the publication of *Madame Bovary*. Ferguson's analysis illustrates how the debate in the courtroom is actually a literary debate over the success and failure of the artistic stature of the novel as a complete and autonomous object. "The defense's argument," Ferguson explains, "is that the novel provides its own judgment, its own punishment to such a degree that there is no need for the courts or anyone else to do a thing.... the novel is complete because it settles its own scores; the tragedy can't grow by an inch or an ounce because Emma has not simply died but has died a death that is a punishment" (750).

47 Most notable in this context is Stanley Fish's "Mission Impossible" chapter in *The Trouble with Principle*.

48 Ferrara, *Justice and Judgment*: "From a certain point of view," Ferrara explains, "the term 'political' seems to acquire a peculiar *anti-political* ring. For a value, a conception of justice, a view of the person and of society, to be 'political' means to be acceptable by everybody by virtue of its being neutral with respect to the divisions that traverse the broader society and culture. The term 'political' takes on the meaning of 'unanimously acceptable,' *au-dessus de la mêlée*. This meaning, intuitively opposite to the one commonly associated with the term 'political,' in fact corresponds to a particular use of the term, which Rawls extends to cover the whole spectrum of the meaning of the term. He uses the term 'political' in a sense comparable to the one which we associate with the adjectives 'constitutional' and 'non-partisan,' usually employed to designate a specific kind of political action—more exquisitely political than partisan politics—ideally associated with the function of the Supreme Court or any similar situation" (22).

49 Bentham, *The Works of Jeremy Bentham*, 496.

50 The obvious and notable exception here is Stephen White's *Edmund Burke*.

51 It is worth emphasizing what seems obvious to many: the fact that both Kant and Burke not only wrote aesthetic treatises on the sublime and the beautiful but also were overwhelmed with the events of the French Revolution. With Kant, the publication of the third critique (1790) coincides with what Hannah Arendt describes as a daily obsession with the events of 1789, when Kant would wait impatiently every day for news of the Revolution (see Arendt, *Lectures on Kant's Political Philosophy*, 44). Although Burke's principal aesthetic work was conceived and written before the French Revolution, that did not stop him from describing the revolution as a sublime event, as I describe in what follows.

52 Burke, *A Philosophical Enquiry*, 57.

53   Also see Slavoj Žižek's discussion of the "sublime object of ideology" in the "Che Vuoi?" chapter of his *Sublime Object of Ideology* for an illuminating account of the sublime.

54   Ferguson, *Solitude and the Sublime*, 8.

55   Burke, *A Philosophical Enquiry*, 57. Note once again Burke's commitment to a Hobbesian view of the state of nature.

56   Burke, *Reflections on the Revolution in France*, 92–93.

57   Ibid., 126–27 (emphasis added).

58   Rancière, *The Names of History*, 24. Note the similarity between Rancière's account of misbegotten speech and Deleuze's description of the sophist, as discussed in chapter 2. In both instances, what counts as "democratic politics" is the inability to speak correctly.

59   Rancière, *The Names of History*, 37.

60   See the chapter "Wrong: Politics and Police," in *Dis-agreement*. I retain the French *tort* (Rancière's term in *La Mésentente*) throughout, as the English "wrong" eludes the significant juridical dimension of tort that, as I suggest, is crucial to the historical and theoretical specificity of Rancière's discussion.

61   Owen, *Philosophical Foundations of Tort Law*, 7.

62   Blackstone, *Commentaries on the Laws of England*, 54. Blackstone explains further that an individual act can exceed the intention of the agent such that an action's value—that is, an agent's liability—must be judged on the basis of its effects. Implicit in Blackstone's account is a description of what he refers to as the *declaratory* aspect of the law, by which he means the instruction of the rules of conduct within any civil order. By combining the remedial with the declaratory, obligation ensues: "Legislators and their laws are said to *compel* and *oblige* . . . because, by declaring and exhibiting a penalty against offenders, they bring it to pass that no man can easily choose to transgress the law; since, by reason of the impending correction, compliance is in high degree preferable to disobedience" (57).

63   I want to stress what the English translation of *La Mésentente: Politique et Philosophie* (Galilée, 1995) omits. Namely, that the term "wrong" in Rancière ought not to be read merely as a judgment on the logical correctness of a proposition (i.e., a mistake) but, moreover, as a historical instance when the notion of *tort* (that is, to be wronged) emerges. In this light, the legal notion of *tort* (as in tort law) is in play in Rancière's treatment of the category of "wrong" in *Dis-agreement*. This is particularly relevant given the fact that tort law as a field of inquiry emerges around the time of the French Revolution, in the latter part of the eighteenth century. I would like to thank Frances Ferguson for mentioning this to me.

64 Rancière, *Dis-agreement*, x.
65 Ibid., xii.
66 Ibid., 4. Although Rancière does not cite it, the appropriate section in question is book 5 of the *Nicomachean Ethics*.
67 Aristotle, *Nicomachean Ethics*, 1133^b32–1134^a08, in *The Complete Works of Aristotle*, vol. 2.
68 Rancière, *Dis-agreement*, 28.
69 Foucault, *The Foucault Effect*, 93. Rancière's treatment of the police is at once indebted to Foucault's discussion of governmentality and a polemic against Louis Althusser's interpellative "Hey, you there!" of the "every day police" from Althusser's "Ideology and Ideological State Apparatuses" (*Lenin and Philosophy*, 174).
70 Howard Caygill reminds us that the term *police* derives from the German *Polizei*, "which was thought to originate in the translation of Aristotle's *Politics*, and was used to describe the administrative innovations of Burgundy and France in the fifteenth century, innovations which were transplanted to the Habsburg court and entered Germany as imperial police-ordinances. The ordinances were issues to meet immediate and specific social problems which were not covered by existing law or custom" (*Art of Judgment*, 104–5). It seems likely that Rancière's contrast of "the police" with "politics" relies on this early modern administrative notion of *Polizeiwissenschaft*. But, Rancière's distinction is more than a historical curiosity. It is, for him, the fulcrum upon which the aesthetics of politics pivots: "I call 'police' the divisions of the sensible that claims to recognize only real parties to the exclusion of all empty spaces and supplements. Society here consists of groups devoted to specific modes of doing, in places where these occupations are performed, and in modes of being that correspond to these occupations and these places. I call 'politics' the mode of acting that perturbs this arrangement by instituting within its perceptual field the contradictory theatre of its 'appearances.' The essence of politics is then dissensus. But dissensus is not the opposition of interests or opinions. It is the production, within a determined, sensible world, of a given that is heterogeneous to it" (*The Philosopher and His Poor*, 226).
71 Rancière, *Dis-agreement*, 29–30.
72 Ibid., 6.
73 Ibid., 50.
74 Ibid.
75 Rancière, *The Philosopher and His Poor*, 226.
76 Rancière, *Dis-agreement*, 99 (emphasis added).
77 Jacques Rancière's commitment to the "scandal of thinking" might

seem like a classic deconstructive move. But it is important to distinguish Rancière's treatment of the limits of representation (i.e., the part of those who have no part) from Jacques Derrida's seemingly similar sentiment. The crucial difference between them is that although both admit to the limits of representation, Rancière is not willing to repudiate representation tout court, as Derrida seems to do at times. That is to say, by pointing to the limits of representation and by representing those limits as a "mistake," Rancière shows both what representations can do and their failures. See his reply to my first question in Panagia, "Dissenting Words," 114.

Chapter 4: Habermas, Hazlitt, and the Essay

1   See Bill Readings's *The University in Ruins* and Allan Bloom's *The Closing of the American Mind.* Consider also this recent statement by Michael Sandel in a *New York Times* report on higher education in America: "If colleges and universities are to be something more than places that provide basic training for the world of work and consumption, they have to concern themselves with larger moral and civic purposes . . . The purpose of higher education is not just to train students to enter the labor market, it is to shape citizens who can participate effectively in democratic life. That means that colleges and universities have to engage moral and civic questions as institutions, beyond the classroom" (Karen W. Arenson, "The Moral Compass on Campus," *New York Times*, June 10, 2001).

2   Montaigne's essays are primarily reflective, representing his thoughts on a variety of topics including love, friendship, death, and commerce—things that pertain to the relationship of one's self to one's life. In the eighteenth and nineteenth centuries, however, the essay shifts emphasis, "developing into a tool that represents the previously unremarked spaces of civil society in their own terms" (S. Black, "Social and Literary Form in the *Spectator*," 25). What distinguishes the Enlightenment essay from its early modern predecessor, then, is its distinctly modern commitment to representing a public by describing the activities occurring in salons, coffeehouses, public squares, and the like.

3   See Locke's "Epistle to the Reader," in *An Essay Concerning Understanding*.

4   Habermas, *The Inclusion of the Other*, 37.

5   Seyla Benhabib explains how freedom is, in fact, the first principle of Habermas's communicative ethics: "*Freedom* means the suspension of

all internal and external constraints of action and the right to follow the 'force' of the better argument only" (*Critique, Norm, and Utopia*, 289).

6   *Oxford English Dictionary*, 2nd ed., s.v. grotesque.
7   Bakhtin, *Rabelais and His World*, 32.
8   Montaigne, *The Complete Essays of Montaigne*, 135.
9   See my discussion of nothingness vis-à-vis Gilles Deleuze's critique of dialectical reasoning in chapter 2.
10 Montaigne, *The Complete Essays of Montaigne*, 135.
11 Ibid., 611.
12 Adorno, "The Essay as Form," in *Notes to Literature*, 16.
13 Ibid., 22.
14 Ibid., 4.
15 Ibid., 18.
16 Ibid., 23.
17 S. Black, "Social and Literary Form in the *Spectator*," 27.
18 Habermas, *Moral Consciousness and Communicative Action*, 135.
19 Ibid., 211.
20 Ibid., 137.
21 Ibid., 136.
22 Ibid., 134.
23 Notable in this regard are Young, "Communication and the Other"; Herrnstein Smith, "The Skeptic's Turn: A Performative Contradiction," in *Belief and Resistance*; Jay, "The Debate over the Performative Contradiction," in *Philosophical Interventions in the Unfinished Project of Modernity*; McCarthy, "The Idea of a Universal Pragmatics," in *The Critical Theory of Jürgen Habermas*; and Martin Morris, "The Performative Contradiction in the Radical Critique of Domination," in *Rethinking the Communicative Turn*.
24 David Hume makes a similar point in his analysis of the obligation of the promise. He explains how the nature of the promise is of the new, and how each promissory utterance creates a new obligation that supposes new sentiments to arise. Because of its inventive, artificial character, there can be no natural grounding for the moral obligation implied in the promise. Rather, the ground is to be found in an interest in society per se. All commerce, exchange, and social interaction is governed by this "certain form of words," and by using these "transubstantiating" incantations, individuals subject themselves "to the penalty of never being trusted again in case of failure" (*A Treatise of Human Nature*, 3.5.336). The invocation of trust as a binding force between individuals in civil society is key. Since Hume

makes it impossible for us to ground moral obligation on anything natural, the only real grounding for the obligations we impose on ourselves is our own free will and our own interest in being trusted by others. The promise, then, is an instance of pure artifice but it is precisely its artificial nature that guarantees the possibility of civil society. The faculty of the imagination thus allows us to represent to ourselves an image of what life would be like if we were to enter into a relation with an other. Because the interest in commerce is not based on friendship, the artifice of the promise is required in order to build trust.

25 Benhabib, *Critique, Norm, and Utopia*, 294–95.
26 Habermas, *Moral Consciousness and Communicative Action*, 100–1.
27 See Polanyi, *Personal Knowledge*.
28 Habermas, *The Structural Transformation of the Public Sphere*, 89. It is worth noting that reputation insists on both a moral and an aesthetic evaluation of an other's character. A judgment of taste thus allows one to determine the value of an other's person, thereby determining further how they will be included in sociopolitical life.
29 Habermas, *The Structural Transformation of the Public Sphere*, 41.
30 For a discussion of the "human situatedness of reason" and Habermas's debt to Hegel, see Benhabib, "In the Shadow of Aristotle and Hegel," in *Situating the Self*. Also see Ferrara, "Democracy, Justice and Discourse," in *Justice and Judgement*.
31 Habermas, *The Structural Transformation of the Public Sphere*, 31.
32 Ibid., 42.
33 Habermas's main example is the debates and discussions that revolved around Samuel Richardson's *Pamela* (1740). Richardson's psychological novel is organized around a series of letters where the main characters reveal themselves through letter writing. In the "literary form" of the letter, individuals discovered the means by which they could reveal the truth of themselves to others: "It is no accident," Habermas explains, "that the eighteenth century became the century of the letter: through letter writing the individual unfolded himself in his subjectivity" (ibid., 48).
34 Habermas, *The Inclusion of the Other*, 37.
35 Habermas, "Further Reflections on the Public Sphere," in *Habermas and the Public Sphere*, 427.
36 See the distinction he makes in the preface of *The Structural Transformation of the Public Sphere*.
37 Habermas, *Habermas and the Public Sphere*, 426.
38 Berlin, *The Roots of Romanticism*, 7.

NOTES TO CHAPTER 4   149

39   Dart, *Rousseau, Robespierre, and English Romanticism*, 173.
40   This is the thesis of Dart's reading of *The Prelude*, 178.
41   Coleridge, "Once a Jacobin Always a Jacobin," in *The Collected Works of Samuel Taylor Coleridge*, 368.
42   Dart, *Rousseau, Robespierre, and English Romanticism*, 215.
43   In "Taking Liberties in Foucault's Triangle," Kirstie McClure makes a similar point, describing Hazlitt's political subject as "prickly," resisting permanent allegiances or social stasis (*Identities, Politics, and Rights*, 125).
44   On Hazlitt's indebtedness to Montaigne, see Bromwich, *Hazlitt*, 345–51.
45   Hazlitt, "On Familiar Style."
46   Ibid.
47   Ibid.
48   Hazlitt, "Malthus," in *Selected Writings*, 79; originally published as *A Reply to the Essay on Population* (1807).
49   Bromwich, *Hazlitt*, 345.
50   Quoted in Dart, *Rousseau, Robespierre, and English Romanticism*, 232.
51   Hazlitt, "On the Pleasure of Hating," in *The Plain Speaker*, 102.
52   Ibid., 102.
53   Ibid., 103.
54   Ibid., 106.
55   Ibid., 106.
56   Hazlitt, "On a Portrait of an English Lady, by Vandyke," in *The Plain Speaker*, 170.
57   "Never have two men judged alike of the same thing," Montaigne asserts, "and it is impossible to find two opinions exactly similar, not only in different men, but in the same man at different times" ("Of Experience," in *The Complete Essays of Montaigne*, 337).
58   "For what is the People? Millions of men, like you, with thoughts stirring in their minds, with the blood circulating in their veins, with wants and appetites, and passions and anxious cares" (Hazlitt, *Selected Writings*, 3).
59   Hazlitt, "The Same Subject Continued," in *The Plain Speaker*, 30.
60   Ibid.
61   Hazlitt, *Selected Writings*, 3.
62   For more on democratic litigiousness, see Jacques Rancière's ninth thesis in "Ten Theses on Politics," as well as Panagia, "Dissenting Words."
63   Herzog, *Poisoning the Minds of the Lower Orders*, 53.

Afterword: *Les Sans Papiers*

I am indebted to Bonnie Honig and Patchen Markell for their attentiveness to earlier versions of this section.

1 The "right of sanctuary" or simply "sanctuary" refers to a consecrated space giving protection to those fleeing from justice or persecution, or the privilege of taking refuge in such consecrated place. This right was based on the inviolability attached to things sacred. It was recognized under the Code of Theodosius (399 AD) and later by that of Justinian. Papal sanction was first given by Leo I in 460, though the first Council of Orange had dealt with the matter in 441 (see "The Catholic Encyclopedia," www.newadvent.org/cathen/13430a.htm). This "right" was most recently and most notoriously invoked by General Noriega in January of 1990 when he took sanctuary in the Papal Nunciature in Panama City, hoping to be granted political asylum from American forces. As is their right, on that occasion church officials refused Noriega sanctuary.

2 See O'Connell's "Plight of France's *Sans-Papiers*."

3 "Statement of the Voiceless."

4 By *anomic* I am referring to both the Latin and Greek etymology of the term *name*: the Latin *anomia* finds its root in *nomen* and refers to the aphasiac condition of not being able to associate a name with its object (or, in this case, a subject). But the Latin *nomen* is itself indebted to the Greek *nomos* (law, custom, manner). *Anomic* thus refers to the suspension of both the linguistic category of *nomen* and the legal category of *nomos*. It is in this sense that we might affirm the perverse tautology of the anomic sans papiers.

5 Foucault, *History of Sexuality*, 88–89.

6 Coupling the idea of authorial intention with sovereign authority, Foucault also makes this a problem of poesis in "What is an Author?" (in *The Foucault Reader*). Especially notable in this regard is the methodological shift that occurs in the two sets of questions in the concluding paragraph.

7 Foucault, *Power/Knowledge*, 108.

8 As Georges Bataille (in "The Psychological Structure of Fascism") and Deleuze and Guattari (in their claim in *A Thousand Plateaus* that we must remain aware of emerging micro-fascisms) have argued, to remain open to the virtual does not imply an endorsement of any and all potentialities.

Bibliography

Adorno, Theodor. *Notes to Literature*. Vol. 1. Ed. Rolf Tiedemann. New York: Columbia University Press, 1991.
Althusser, Louis. *Lenin and Philosophy and Other Essays*. New York: Monthly Review Press, 1971.
Anderson, Amanda. "Pragmatism and Character." *Critical Inquiry* 29 (2003): 283–301.
Arendt, Hannah. *The Human Condition*. Chicago: University of Chicago Press, 1958.
———. *Between Past and Future*. New York: Penguin Books, 1977.
———. *Lectures on Kant's Political Philosophy*. Ed. Ronal Beiner. Chicago: University of Chicago Press, 1989.
Aristotle. *The Complete Works of Aristotle*. Ed. Jonathan Barnes. Vols. 1 and 2. Bollingen Series. Princeton, N.J.: Princeton University Press, 1984.
Auerbach, Eric. *Scenes from the Drama of European Literatures: Six Essays*. Gloucester, Mass: P. Smith, 1973.
Augustine, Bishop of Hippo. *Confessions*. New York: Oxford University Press, 1994.
Badiou, Alain. *Deleuze: La clameur de l'Etre*. Paris: Hachette, 1997.
Bakhtin, Mikhail. *Rabelais and His World*. Bloomington: Indiana University Press, 1984.
Baltrusaitis, J. *Anamorphic Art*. Cambridge: Chadwyck-Healey, Ltd., 1977.
Barthes, Roland. *Image-Music-Text*. Trans. Stephen Heath. New York: Hill and Wang, 1988.

Benhabib, Seyla. *Critique, Norm, and Utopia*. New York: Columbia University Press, 1986.

———. *Situating the Self: Gender, Community, and Postmodernism in Contemporary Ethics*. New York: Routledge, 1992.

———, ed. *Democracy and Difference: Contesting the Boundaries of the Political*. Princeton, N.J.: Princeton University Press, 1998.

Bennett, Jane. *The Enchantment of Modern Life: Attachments, Crossings, Ethics*. Princeton, N.J.: Princeton University Press, 2001.

Bentham, Jeremy. *The Works of Jeremy Bentham*. Vol. 2. Ed. Sir John Bowring. London: Simpkin, Marshall, 1843.

Berlin, Isaiah. *Four Essays on Liberty*. London: Oxford University Press, 1992.

———. *The Roots of Romanticism*. Princeton, N.J.: Princeton University Press, 1999.

Black, Scott. "Social and Literary Form in the *Spectator*." *Eighteenth-Century Studies* 33.1 (1999): 21–42.

Blackstone, William. *Commentaries on the Laws of England*. Vol. 1. Chicago: University of Chicago Press, 1979.

Blair, Ann. "Annotating and Indexing Natural Philosophy." In *Books and the Sciences in History*, ed. Nicholas Jardine and Marina Frasca-Spada. New York: Cambridge University Press, 2000.

Bloom, Allan. *The Closing of the American Mind*. New York: Touchstone Books, 1988.

Böhrer, Karl Heinz. *Suddenness: On the Moment of Aesthetic Appearance*. Trans. Ruth Crowley. New York: Columbia University Press, 1994.

Borges, Jorge Luis. *Labyrinths*. New York: New Directions Publishers, 1964.

Bourdieu, Pierre. *Rules of Art: Genesis and Structure of the Literary Field*. Palo Alto, Calif.: Stanford University Press, 1996.

Bromwich, David. *Hazlitt: The Mind of a Critic*. New York: Oxford University Press, 1983.

Bruns, Gerald. *Heidegger's Estrangements: Language, Truth, and Poetry in the Later Writings*. New Haven, Conn: Yale University Press, 1989.

Burke, Edmund. *A Philosophical Enquiry into the Origins of our Ideas of the Sublime and Beautiful*. Ed. James T. Boulton. London: University of Notre Dame Press, 1986.

Burke, Edmund. *Reflections on the Revolution in France*. London: Penguin Classics, 1986.

Camille, Michael. *Master of Death: The Lifeless Art of Pierre Remiet Illuminator*. New Haven, Conn.: Yale University Press, 1996.

Caygill, Howard. *The Art of Judgment*. Oxford: Basil Blackwell, 1989.
Cicero. *De Oratore III*. Trans. H. Rackham. Loeb Classical Library, vol. 4. Cambridge, Mass.: Harvard University Press, 1992.
Cohen, Peter. *The Architecture of Doom*. First Run Features, 1991.
Coleridge, Samuel Taylor. *The Collected Works of Samuel Taylor Coleridge*. Bollingen Series, ed. David V. Erdman. Princeton, N.J.: Princeton University Press, 1990.
Colie, Rosalie. *Paradoxia Epidemica*. Princeton, N.J.: Princeton University Press, 1966.
Colletti, Lucio. *Marxism and Hegel*. Trans. Lawrence Garner. London: Verso, 1979.
Coppe, Abeizer. *Selected Writings*. London: Aporia, 1987.
Corbett, Margery, and Lightbown, R. W. *The Comely Frontispiece: The Emblematic Title-Page in England, 1550–1660*. London: Routledge and Kegan Paul, 1979.
Cornell, Drucilla. *Defending Ideals*. New York: Routledge, 2004.
Dart, Gregory. *Rousseau, Robespierre and English Romanticism*. Cambridge: Cambridge University Press, 1999.
Daston, Lorraine, and Park, Katherine. *Wonders and the Order of Nature*. New York: Zone Books, 1998.
Deleuze, Gilles. *The Logic of Sense*. Trans. Mark Lester and Charles Stivale. New York: Columbia University Press, 1990.
———. *Kant's Critical Philosophy*. Trans. Hugh Tomlinson and Barbara Habberjam. Minneapolis: University of Minnesota Press, 1993.
———. *Difference and Repetition*. Trans. Paul Patton. New York: Columbia University Press, 1994.
———. *Essays: Critical and Clinical*. Minneapolis: University of Minnesota Press, 1997.
———. *Expressionism in Philosophy: Spinoza*. Trans. Martin Joughin. New York: Zone Books, 1997.
Deleuze, Gilles, and Guattari, Félix. *A Thousand Plateaus*. Trans. Brian Massumi. Minneapolis: University of Minnesota Press, 1993.
———. *What Is Philosophy?* Trans. Hugh Tomlinson and Graham Burchell. European Perspectives, ed. Lawrence D. Kritzman. New York: Columbia University Press, 1994.
Derrida, Jacques. *Writing and Difference*. Trans. Alan Bass. Chicago: University of Chicago Press, 1978.
Derrida, Jacques. *Margins of Philosophy*. Trans. Alan Bass. Chicago: University of Chicago Press, 1982.

———. *Dissemination*. Trans. Barbara Johnson. Chicago: University of Chicago Press, 1983.
———. *Of Grammatology*. Trans. Gayatri Spivak. Baltimore: Johns Hopkins University Press, 1998.
Drucker, Fred. *The Practice of Management*. New York: Harper Business, 1993.
Dryden, John. *Essays of Dryden*. Ed. W. P. Ker. Vol. 1. New York: Russel and Russel, 1961.
Duns Scotus, John. *Duns Scotus, Metaphysician*. Ed. William A. Frank and Allan B. Wolter. West Lafayette, Ind.: Purdue University Press, 1995.
Euripides. *The Suppliants*. E. P. Coleridge translation. http://etext.library.adelaide.edu.au/e/e8/suppliants.html (accessed Feb. 21, 2003).
Ferguson, Frances. *Solitude and the Sublime*. New York: Routledge, 1992.
———. "Emma, or Happiness (or Sex Work)." *Critical Inquiry* 28 (2002): 749-79.
———. *Pornography, the Theory: What Utilitarianism Did to Action*. Chicago: University of Chicago Press, 2004.
Ferrara, Alessandro. *Justice and Judgement: The Rise and Prospect of the Judgment Model in Contemporary Political Thought*. Newbury Park, Calif.: Sage Publications, 1999.
Fish, Stanley. *Surprised by Sin: The Reader in Paradise Lost*. New York: St. Martin's Press, 1967.
———. *Doing What Comes Naturally: Change, Rhetoric and the Practice of Theory in Literary and Legal Studies*. Durham, N.C.: Duke University Press, 1989.
———. *The Trouble with Principle*. Cambridge, Mass.: Harvard University Press, 2000.
Fisher, Philip. *The Vehement Passions*. Princeton, N.J.: Princeton University Press, 2003.
Flathman, Richard E. "Book Review of Skinner's Reason and Rhetoric in the Philosophy of Hobbes." *Ethics* 108 (1998): 820-23.
Foucault, Michel. *Language, Counter-Memory, Practice: Selected Essays and Interviews*. Trans. Donald Bouchard and Sherry Simon. Ithaca, N.Y.: Cornell University Press, 1977.
———. *Power/Knowledge: Selected Interviews and Other Writings, 1972–1977*. Ed. Colin Gordon. New York: Pantheon, 1980.
———. *The Foucault Reader*. Ed. Paul Rabinow. New York: Pantheon, 1984.
———. *The History of Sexuality: An Introduction*. New York: Vintage Books, 1990.
———. *The Foucault Effect: Studies in Governmentality*. Ed. Graham Bur-

chell, Colin Gordon, and Peter Miller. Chicago: University of Chicago Press, 1991.
———. *The Order of Things: An Archaeology of the Human Sciences*. New York: Vintage Books, 1994.
Fried, Michael. *Art and Objecthood*. Chicago: University of Chicago Press, 1998.
Frye, Northrop. *Anatomy of Criticism*. Princeton, N.J.: Princeton University Press, 1957.
Gadamer, Hans-Georg. *Truth and Method*. Trans. Joel Weinsheimer and Donald Marshall. 2nd rev. ed. New York: Continuum, 1993.
Gilman, Ernest. *The Curious Perspective*. New Haven, Conn.: Yale University Press, 1978.
Ginzburg, Carlo. *The Cheese and the Worms*. Baltimore: Johns Hopkins University Press, 1980.
Greenblatt, Stephen. *Renaissance Self-Fashioning: From More to Shakespeare*. Chicago: University of Chicago Press, 1980.
Guillory, John. *Cultural Capital: The Problem of Literary Canon Formation*. Chicago: University of Chicago Press, 1993.
Gutmann, Amy. *Democratic Education*. Princeton, N.J.: Princeton University Press, 1987.
Habermas, Jürgen. *The Philosophical Discourse of Modernity*. Cambridge, Mass.: MIT Press, 1987.
———. *Moral Consciousness and Communicative Action*. Trans. Christian Lenhardt and Shierry Weber Nicholsen. Cambridge, Mass.: MIT Press, 1990.
———. "Further Reflections on the Public Sphere." In *Habermas and the Public Sphere*, ed. Craig Calhoun. Cambridge, Mass.: MIT Press, 1992.
———. "The Rawls/Habermas Exchange." *Journal of Philosophy* 92 (1995): 109.
———. *Postmetaphysical Thinking*. Trans. William M. Hohengarten. Cambridge, Mass.: MIT Press, 1996.
———. *The Structural Transformation of the Public Sphere*. Trans. Thomas Burger. Cambridge, Mass.: MIT Press, 1996.
———. *The Inclusion of the Other*. Ed. Ciaran Cronin and Pablo De Greiff. Cambridge, Mass.: MIT Press, 1998.
Hazlitt, William. "On Familiar Style." *Table Talk, Essays on Men and Manners* (1822). http://www.blupete.com/Literature/Essays/Hazlitt/TableTalk/FamiliarStyle.htm (accessed Sept. 13, 2003).
———. *Selected Writings*. Ed. Jon Cook. New York: Oxford University Press, 1995.

———. *The Plain Speaker: Ten Key Essays*. Ed. Duncan Wu. London: Blackwell, 1998.

Heidegger, Martin. *Poetry, Language, Thought*. Trans. Albert Hofstadter. New York: Harper and Row, 1971.

Herzog, Don. *Poisoning the Minds of the Lower Orders*. Princeton, N.J.: Princeton University Press, 1998.

Hobbes, Thomas. "To the Readers." Preface to Thucydides, *The Peloponnesian War*, trans. Thomas Hobbes. Chicago: University of Chicago Press, 1989.

———. *Leviathan*. Cambridge Texts in the History of Political Thought, ed. Quentin Skinner, Raymond Geuss, and Richard Tuck. Cambridge: Cambridge University Press, 1992.

———. "A Discourse upon *Gondibert*." In *The Later Renaissance in England*, ed. Herschel Baker. New York: Waveland Press, 1995.

Honig, Bonnie. *Democracy and the Foreigner*. Princeton, N.J.: Princeton University Press, 2003.

Hume, David. *A Treatise of Human Nature*. Oxford: Clarendon, 1978.

———. *An Enquiry Concerning the Principles of Morals*. Ed. Jerome Schneewind. Indianapolis: Hackett, 1983.

———. *Essays: Moral, Political, and Literary*. Ed. Eugene F. Miller. Indianapolis: Liberty Classics, 1987.

Hunter, Ian. "Aesthetics and Cultural Studies." In *Cultural Studies*, ed. Lawrence Grossberg, Cary Nelson, and Paula A. Treichler. New York: Routledge, 1992.

Jabès, Edmund. *A Foreigner Carrying in the Crook of His Arm a Tiny Book*. Trans. Rosmarie Waldrop. Hanover, N.H.: Wesleyan University Press, 1993.

Jay, Martin. *Philosophical Interventions in the Unfinished Project of Modernity*. Cambridge, Mass.: MIT Press, 1992.

Johnston, David. *The Rhetoric of Leviathan: Thomas Hobbes and the Politics of Cultural Transformation*. Princeton, N.J.: Princeton University Press, 1989.

Kant, Immanuel. *Kant's Political Writings*. Ed. Hans Reiss. London: Cambridge University Press, 1970.

———. *Critique of Judgment*. Trans. Werner Pluhar. Indianapolis: Hackett, 1987.

———. *Critique of Practical Reason*. Trans. Lewis White Beck. 3rd ed. Toronto: Macmillan/Library of Liberal Arts, 1993.

Kaplan, Robert. *The Nothing That Is: A Natural History of Zero*. New York: Oxford University Press, 1999.

Kompridis, Nikolas. "Amidst the Plurality of Voices: Philosophy of Music after Adorno." *Angelaki* 8.3 (2003): 167–80.

Kripke, Saul. *Naming and Necessity*. Cambridge, Mass.: Harvard University Press, 1982.

Larmore, Charles. *The Morals of Modernity*. New York: Cambridge University Press, 1997.

Locke, John. *An Essay Concerning Understanding*. Kent: Wordsworth Classics, 1998.

Lyon, Janet. *Manifestoes: Provocations of the Modern*. Ithaca, N.Y.: Cornell University Press, 1999.

Lyotard, Jean-François. *Lessons on the Analytic of the Sublime*. Palo Alto, Calif.: Stanford University Press, 1994.

Macksey, Richard, and Eugenio Donato. *The Languages of Criticism and the Sciences of Man: The Structuralist Controversy*. Baltimore: Johns Hopkins University Press, 1970.

Malcolm, Noel. *Aspects of Hobbes*. New York: Oxford University Press, 2002.

Markell, Patchen. *Bound by Recognition*. Princeton, N.J.: Princeton University Press, 2003.

The Matrix. Dir. Andy Wachowski and Larry Wachowski. Warner Bros., 1997.

McCarthy, Thomas. *The Critical Theory of Jürgen Habermas*. Cambridge, Mass.: MIT Press, 1981.

McClure, Kirstie. "Taking Liberties in Foucault's Triangle." *Identities, Politics, and Rights*, ed. Austin Sarat and Thomas R. Kearns. Ann Arbor: University of Michigan Press, 1995.

———. "The Odor of Judgment: Exemplarity, Propriety, and Politics in the Company of Hannah Arendt." In *Hannah Arendt and the Meaning of Politics*, ed. Craig Calhoun and John McGowan. Minneapolis: University of Minnesota Press, 1997.

McKeon, R. *Rhetoric: Essays in Invention and Discovery*. Ed. Mark Backman. Woodbridge, Conn.: Ox Box, 1987.

Michaels, Walter Benn. *Our America: Nativism, Modernism, and Pluralism*. Durham, N.C.: Duke University Press, 1995.

———. "Political Science Fictions." *New Literary History* 31 (2000): 649–64.

———. *The Shape of the Signifier*. Princeton, N.J.: Princeton University Press, 2004.

Montaigne, Michel de. *The Complete Essays*. Ed. Donald Frame. Palo Alto, Calif.: Stanford University Press, 1990.

Morris, Martin. *Rethinking the Communicative Turn*. New York: SUNY Press, 2001.

Musil, Robert. *The Man without Qualities*. Vol. 1. New York: Vintage Books, 1996.

Nietzsche, Friedrich. *The Will to Power*. New York: Vintage Books, 1989.

Nussbaum, Martha. *Love's Knowledge*. London: Oxford University Press, 1990.

———. *Poetic Justice: The Literary Imagination and Public Life*. New York: Beacon, 1997.

———. "The Professor of Parody: The Hip Defeatism of Judith Butler." *New Republic*, February 22, 1999, 37–45.

Oakeshott, Michael. *Rationalism in Politics*. Indianapolis: Liberty, 1992.

O'Connell, Christian. "Plight of France's *Sans-Papiers* Gives a Face to Struggle Over Immigration Reform." *Human Rights Brief* 4.1 (1996). http://www.wcl.american.edu/hrbrief/v4i1/pasqua41.htm (accessed Dec. 2003).

Owen, David, ed. *Philosophical Foundations of Tort Law*. Oxford: Clarendon, 1995.

Panagia, Davide. "The Predicative Function in Ideology." *Journal of Political Ideologies* 6.1 (2001): 55–74.

Panagia, Davide, and Jacques Rancière. "Dissenting Words: A Conversation with Jacques Rancière." *Diacritics* 30 (summer 2000): 113–26.

Pearson, Keith Ansell. *Germinal Life: The Difference and Repetition of Deleuze*. New York: Routledge, 1999.

Pitkin, Hanna F. *The Concept of Representation*. Los Angeles: University of California Press, 1972.

Plato. *The Republic*. New York: Norton, 1985.

Poison. "Every Rose Has Its Thorn." On *Open Up and Say . . . Ahh!*. Capitol Records, 1988.

Polanyi, Michael. *Personal Knowledge: Towards a Post-Critical Philosophy*. Chicago: University of Chicago Press, 1974.

Quine, W. V. O. "Paradox." *Scientific American* 206 (1962): 84–96.

Rancière, Jacques. *The Names of History: On the Poetics of Knowledge*. Trans. Hassan Melehy. Minneapolis: University of Minnesota Press, 1994.

———. *La Mésentente: Politique et Philosophie*. Paris: Galilée, 1995.

———. *Dis-agreement: Politics and Philosophy*. Trans. Julie Rose. Minneapolis: University of Minnesota Press, 1998.

———. "Ten Theses on Politics." *theory&event* 5.3 (2001) (available online via Project Muse).

———. *The Philosopher and His Poor*. Durham, N.C.: Duke University Press, 2004.
Rawls, John. *A Theory of Justice*. Cambridge, Mass.: Belknap Press of Harvard University Press, 1981.
———. *Political Liberalism*. New York: Columbia University Press, 1993.
———. *Collected Papers*. Ed. Samuel Freeman. Cambridge, Mass.: Harvard University Press, 1999.
———. *Lectures on the History of Moral Philosophy*. Cambridge, Mass.: Harvard University Press, 2000.
Rawls, John, and Jürgen Habermas. "An Exchange." *Journal of Philosophy* 92.3 (1995): 109–31.
Readings, Bill. *The University in Ruins*. Cambridge, Mass.: Harvard University Press, 1996.
Rée, Jonathan. "The Translation of Philosophy." *New Literary History* 32 (2001): 223–57.
Ricoeur, Paul. *Hermeneutics and the Human Sciences*. Trans. John B. Thompson. Cambridge: Cambridge University Press, 1985.
———. *The Rule of Metaphor: Multidisciplinary Studies of the Creation of Meaning in Language*. Toronto: University of Toronto Press, 1987.
———. *Time and Narrative*. 3 vols. Chicago: University of Chicago Press, 1990.
Rotman, Brian. *Signifying Nothing: The Semiotics of Zero*. London: Macmillan Press, 1987.
Rowlands, John. *Holbein: The Paintings of Hans Holbein the Younger*. London: David R. Godine, 1985.
Schoolman, Morton. *Reason and Horror*. New York: Routledge, 2001.
Shapin, Steven, and Schaffer, Simon. *Leviathan and the Air-Pump: Hobbes, Boyle and the Experimental Life*. Princeton, N.J.: Princeton University Press, 1985.
Sharpe, Kevin, and Zwicker, Steven, eds. *Refiguring Revolutions*. Berkeley: University of California Press, 1998.
Shklar, Judith. "The Liberalism of Fear." In *Liberalism and the Moral Life*, ed. Nancy Rosenblum. Cambridge, Mass.: Harvard University Press, 1989.
Shuger, Debora K. *Sacred Rhetoric: The Christian Grand Style in the English Renaissance*. Princeton, N.J.: Princeton University Press, 1988.
Skinner, Quentin. *Reason and Rhetoric in the Philosophy of Hobbes*. New York: Cambridge University Press, 1996.
———. "Hobbes and the Purely Artificial Person of the State." *Journal of Political Philosophy* 7.1 (1999): 1–29.

Skocpol, Theda. *States and Social Revolutions*. Chicago: University of Chicago Press, 1979.
Smith, Barbara Herrnstein. *Belief and Resistance*. Cambridge, Mass.: Harvard University Press, 1997.
"Statement of the Voiceless, Porto Alégre (Brazil) 26/01/2003." http://www.novox.ras.eu.org/doc/NoVoInt_Declaration26janv2003.rtf (accessed Dec. 2003).
Strong, Tracy B. "How to Write Scripture: Words, Authority, and Politics in Thomas Hobbes." *Critical Inquiry* 20 (1993): 128-59.
Thomas, Francis-Noël, and Mark Turner. *Clear and Simple as the Truth*. Princeton, N.J.: Princeton University Press, 1994.
Thucydides. *The Peloponnesian War*. The Complete Hobbes Translation. Chicago: University of Chicago Press, 1989.
Tuck, Richard. *Philosophy and Government: 1572-1651*. Ideas in Context. New York: Cambridge University Press, 1993.
Warner, Michael. *Publics and Counterpublics*. Cambridge, Mass.: Zone Books, 2002.
White, Stephen. *Edmund Burke: Modernity, Politics, and Aesthetics*. Thousand Oaks, Calif.: Sage, 1994.
Wolin, Richard. *The Terms of Cultural Criticism*. New York: Columbia University Press, 1995.
Wolin, Sheldon. *Politics and Vision*. Boston: Little, Brown and Co., 1960.
———. "Review Essay: The Liberal/Democratic Divide: On Rawls's *Political Liberalism*" *Political Theory* 24.1 (1996): 97-119.
Young, Iris Marion. "Communication and the Other." In *Democracy and Difference: Contesting the Boundaries of the Political*, ed. Seyla Benhabib. Princeton, N.J.: Princeton University Press, 1998.
Yunis, Harvey. *Taming Democracy: Models of Political Rhetoric in Classical Athens*. Ithaca, N.Y.: Cornell University Press, 1996.
Žižek, Slavoj. *The Sublime Object of Ideology*. London: Verso, 1989.
———. "The King Is a Thing." *New Formations* 13 (1991): 19-37.

Index

Adorno, Theodor, 100–101, 138 n. 59
Æmilius Porta, 32
Aestheticization of politics thesis, 6, 126 n. 11
Aesthetico-philosophic triplet, 51–54
Aesthetics, 85, 126 n. 11; defined, 4–5; ethics of, 9–17, 101; politics and, 1–8; subjectivity and, 126–27 n. 12. *See also* Aestheticization of politics thesis; Aesthetics of transgression; Kant, Immanuel: aesthetics of; Liberalism: aesthetic value and; Plato: aesthetics of; Rawls, John: aesthetics of; Tort, aesthetics of
Aesthetics of transgression, 14; Rancière and, 93
Agrippa, Cornelius, 29
Althusser, Louis, 91
Ambassadors, The (1533), 27–30, 46, 131–32 n. 29, 132 n. 31
Anamorphosis, 30, 31, 32, 33, 35, 37, 44, 132 n. 32

Anarchical Fallacies (Bentham), 84
Apel, Karol-Otto, 104
Arendt, Hannah, 1, 7, 68, 69, 78, 139 n. 3, 143 n. 51
Argument, 107–8; community and, 106–7; epistemology of, 78–79, 95; function of value in, 139 n. 5; political, 94, 97, 101–2
Aristotle, 5, 50, 90; on good and evil, 137 n. 43; on metaphor, 133 n. 52
"Art and Objecthood" (Fried), 75
Augustine, 58

Badiou, Alain, 58–59, 137 n. 45
Baillet, Adrien, 19, 43
Bakhtin, Mikhail, 47, 48, 109
Beardsley, Monroe, 7
Being, univocity and, 56, 58–60, 137 n. 47
Benhabib, Seyla, 104; on freedom, 146–47 n. 5
Bentham, Jeremy, 84, 111, 112, 128 n. 21
Berlin, Isaiah, 24

Blaberon, 90–92; political, 92
Black, Max, 7
Blackstone, William, 89, 144 n. 62
Burke, Edmund, 84–87, 109, 143 n. 51; on astonishment, 85
Butler, Judith, 10–13

Camille, Michael, 57
Camus, Albert, 66, 67
Carroll, Lewis, 66, 67; on affirmation, 66
Coleridge, Samuel Taylor, 109–10
Colie, Rosalie, 49
Constant, Benjamin, 19, 20, 43
Contemplation, 64
Cornell, Drucilla, 80, 142 n. 39
"Crisis of interpretation," 97
Critique of Judgment (Kant), 16, 69, 70, 74–75, 83
Critique of Practical Reason (Kant), 73, 75
C.S.I., 11
Cypher, 125–26 n. 4

Declaration of the Rights of Man and the Citizen (1791), 84
Deleuze, Gilles, 2, 13–14, 15–16, 138 n. 55, 144 n. 58, 150 n. 8; on aesthetico-philosophic triplet, 51–54; on "banality of the negative," 46; on being and non-being, 65; on "dark precursor," 138–39 n. 60; on demonic participation, 54–56; on dialectics, 60–67; on judgment, 66, 67, 139–40 n. 7; on language as starting point of thinking, 64–65; Nietzsche likened to, 138 n. 59; non-teleological conception of difference, 61–62, 67; on overturning (reversal of) Platonism, 46, 51, 52–56, 65, 136 n. 27; on paradoxes, 47, 63–64; on participation, 135 n. 22, 136 n. 32; on philosophical propositions, 62; on political thinking, 55–56, 61–63, 64, 67; on potentiality, 65; on resemblance, 52–53; on thinking as *creatio*, 63; on univocity of Being, 56, 58–60, 137 n. 47
Democracy, 123–24; dissymmetry and, 84–95; equality and, 122–23; metaphysics and, 8, 77, 83
Derrida, Jacques, 12, 129 n. 29, 136 n. 27, 141 n. 35, 145–46 n. 77; on logocentrism, 54
Dialectics, 52, 135 n. 18; banality of, 60–67
Difference, 46, 60, 138 n. 59; anti-essentialist critiques of, 127–28 n. 18; in itself, 8, 67; qualitative, 14. *See also* Deleuze, Gilles: non-teleological conception of difference
Difference and Repetition (Deleuze), 59, 67, 137 n. 47
Dis-Agreement (Rancière), 91, 92
Discourse ethics, 103–4
Discrimen, 38, 39, 42, 66
Disequality, 122–23
Dryden, John, 25, 33; on translation, 132 n. 41
Duns Scotus, John, 58–60, 63; on God, 58

Erasmus, Desiderius, 29, 97
Essais (Montaigne), 97, 98
Essay Concerning Understanding (Locke), 97
Essay writing, 97, 101, 107, 112, 146 n. 2; discontinuity and, 100; idea of grotesque (*grotesco*) and, 98–100; polemics and, 116–17; political argument and, 97
Ethics, 121, 129 n. 29; dialogical,

97; in hermeneutic experience, 129 n. 36; of problematic, 61. *See also* Aesthetics: ethics of
Euripides, 128 n. 19
Evaluation, culture of, 9-10
Every Rose Has Its Thorn, 7, 127 n.13
Exemplarity, 80-81, 142 n. 144

Ferguson, Frances, 74, 85-86, 128 n. 21, 142-43 n. 46
Ferrara, Alessandro, 83-84; on the "political," 143 n. 48
Fish, Stanley, 50-51
Flathman, Richard, 33
Foucault, Michel, 14, 67, 91, 122, 145 n. 69, 150 n. 6; on aesthetics of transgression, 14
French Revolution, 84, 85, 86-87, 143 n. 51
Fried, Michael, 75. *See also* Rawls, John: aesthetics of
Frye, Northrop, 5

Gadamer, Hans-Georg, 7, 101; hermeneutics of, 126-27 n. 12
Galileo, 31
Ginzburg, Carlo, 134-35 n. 8
Greenblatt, Stephen, 30, 132 n. 30
Grotesque, 47-48, 98-100
Guattari, Félix, 150 n. 8

Habermas, Jürgen, 68, 118, 126n. 11, 130 n. 5, 148 n. 33; on agreement, 102-3; on argument and community, 106-7; on art critics, 106; on communicative action, 102-3, 104, 108, 136 n. 32; on conversation vs. argument, 107-8; on democratic criticism, 107-8; on high vs. low culture, 108-9; on moral theory, 102; performative contradiction and, 104-6, 108, 114, 117; on sincerity and mutual trust in discourse ethics, 103; on validity claims, 102-5
Hazlitt, William, 17, 97, 110-11; essay style of, 112-13; on hatred, 113-15; on legitimacy, 117-18; on portrait painting, 115-16; on sympathy, 111; on utilitarianism, 111-12
Hegel, G. W. F., 60, 61
Heidegger, Martin, 126-27 n. 12
Herzog, Don, 118
Hobbes, Thomas, 14-16, 124, 130-31 n. 14, 131 n. 21, 133 n. 48; barbarism feared by, 31; "barbarity" metaphor and, 21, 33; Cold War reading of, 24; on conscience, 41, 42; on deliberation, 43; empiricism of, 130 n. 13; on etymology of "person," 39; freedom defined by, 40; on immutability of laws of nature, 31, 32; on judgment, 37-38; on knowledge, 40-42; mistranslations of, 41-42; on moral philosophy, 31-32; on "negative liberty," 24, 43; nominalism of, 23, 33, 130 n. 10; *nosce teipsum* translation and, 21-22, 34, 35, 41; optics as interest of, 15, 26, 31; on perspectivism, 26-27, 30, 31; on representation, 15, 22, 38-39, 42, 132 n. 32; on science of politics, 40, 42, 44, 133-34 n. 62; on sovereign, 39-40, 46; as stylist, 25-26, 43; "theatrical production" metaphor and, 37; theory of government of, 23-24; on translation, 26-27, 32-33, 35. *See also* Anamorphosis
Holbein, Hans (the Younger), 27, 29, 31, 40, 46, 132 n. 30
Honig, Bonnie, 10, 125-26 n. 4

Hume, David, 13, 70, 81; on obligation of the promise, 147-48 n. 24

Ideas, 2-3; materiality of, 64-67
Ideology, 1
Imitation, 98-99
Information overload, 20

Jabès, Edmund, 44-45
"Jacobinism," 113
Jacobins, 109-10, 113
Judgment, 68-69; of beauty, 71-72; determinative, 70; reflective, 70, 78
Justice, 54-55, 81-83, 90, 125 n. 4

Kant, Immanuel, 16, 69, 84, 140 n. 9, 140-41 n. 19, 143 n. 51; aesthetics of, 70-75, 81-82, 102, 140 n. 16
Kaplan, Robert, 56-57

Lamb, Charles, 116
Larmore, Charles, 6
L'art pour l'art movement, 126 n. 11
Leviathan (Hobbes), 15, 21, 22, 23, 24, 25, 31, 43, 130-31 n. 14; frontispiece of, 35-37, 133 n. 48; metaphor used in, 26
Liberalism, 24, 27, 123, 142 n. 40; aesthetic value and, 70-84; neo-Kantian, 91-92; utilitarianism and, 69
Liberal/poststructural debate, 2, 97
"Lifeworld," 101-2
Locke, John, 97
Logic of Sense, The (Deleuze), 59-60, 66, 67

Madame Bovary (Flaubert), 142-43 n. 46
Malcolm, Noel, 25, 132 n.32

Malthus, Thomas, 112
Matrix, The, 125 n. 4
Mersenne circle, 26, 30, 31
Mésentente, 89-90
Metaphor, 7-8, 85
Michaels, Walter Benn, 127-28 n. 18
Milton, John, 50-51
Mimesis, 121, 122, 123, 124. *See also* Representation: mimetic
Montaigne, Michel de, 48, 96, 97, 146 n. 2, 149 n. 57; grotesque appreciated by, 98-100
Moral image of thought, 10
Moral philosophy, 31-32, 102
More, Thomas, 29
Musil, Robert, 1

Negation/affirmation paradox, 48
Nicomachean Ethics (Aristotle), 90
Nietzsche, Friedrich, 138 n. 58
No vox movement, 120, 122
Nominalism, 130 n. 10
Nosce teipsum, 21-22, 34, 35, 41
Nothingness, 56-60
Nussbaum, Martha, 10-13, 14, 129 n. 26, 129 n. 29; on human flourishing, 13; on ideology of allegory, 13; on metaphorical imagination, 13, 129 n. 30; on the novel, 12; on perceptive equilibrium, 12; on qualitative difference, 12

Oakeshott, Michael, 25, 43
"Of Experience" (Montaigne), 116
"Of Friendship" (Montaigne), 98
Of the Standard of Taste (Hume), 13
Optics, 29, 30. *See also* Hobbes, Thomas: optics as interest of

Pamela (Richardson), 130 n. 5, 148 n. 33

Paradise Lost (Milton), 50–51
Paradoxes, 48–50, 63–64, 77, 138 n. 59; as *ars rhetorica*, 49
Park, Katherine, 134 n. 3
Pasqua Laws, 119–20
Peloponnesian Wars (Thucydides, trans. T. Hobbes), 26, 32, 43–44
Performative contradiction, 103–8
Philosophical Enquiry into the Origin of our Ideas of the Sublime and Beautiful (Burke), 84–85
Philosophy, 62; obscurity in, 129 n. 26; rhetoric and, 49–51, 135 n. 13
Pinsky, L. E., 135 n. 11
Pitkin, Hanna, 25, 42
Pitt, William, 109
Plain Speaker, The (Hazlitt), 112
Plato, 3–4, 46, 51, 53, 128 n. 20, 136 n. 27; aesthetics of, 51–52, 54; distrust of aesthetics and, 5; on justice, 54–55, 125 n. 4. *See also* Deleuze, Gilles: on overturning (reversal of) Platonism
Platonism, 46, 51, 52–56, 65, 136 n. 27
Pluralism, 8, 47
Poetics, 126–27 n. 12. *See also* Political thought: poetics of
Poetics (Aristotle), 5, 133 n. 52
Poison, 7, 127 n. 13
Polanyi, Michael, 105
Political Essays (Locke), 111, 113
Political Liberalism (Rawls), 76
Political theory, literary competence and, 6, 10, 96–98
Political thought, 3, 20, 34, 94, 97–98, 102; defined, 2–3; forms of representation and, 4–6, 22–23, 35; image and, 2–4; judgment and, 68–69; Pauline conversion experience and, 123; poetics of, 5, 6, 8, 14, 92–93, 121, 124. *See also* Deleuze, Gilles: on political thinking; Rancière, Jacques: on political thinking; Rawls, John: on political thinking
Politics, 91, 92, 142 n. 40, 145 n. 70; consensus, 123; democratic, 88, 92–94, 123; geometry and, 133–34 n. 62; identity, 127–28 n. 18; science of, 32
Politics (Aristotle), 145 n. 70
Praise of Folly (Erasmus), 29
"Principle of publicity," 106

Quine, W. V. O., 48–49
Quintilian, 34, 38, 39

Rabelais, François, 47–48
Rabelais and His World (Bakhtin), 47, 108
Rancière, Jacques, 16, 20, 69, 119, 144 n. 58; on Althusser's police, 91; on *blaberon*, 90–91; on democratic politics and the sublime, 88; on limits of representation, 145–46 n. 77; on mésentente, 89–90; on the no-part, 92; on police vs. politics, 91, 145 n. 69, 145 n. 70; on political thinking, 93–95; on the term "wrong," 144 n. 60, 144 n. 63
Rawls, John, 5, 14, 16, 27, 68–69, 143 n. 48; aesthetics of, 75–84; on deliberation, 77–78, 82–83; on *l'art pour l'art*, 83; on political culture, 76; "political liberalism" of, 82–84; on political paradox, 77; on political thinking, 92–95; on representability, 79–80; on shape and framework of thought, 75; sympathy and, 81
Rée, Jonathan, 79, 129 n. 26; on problem of voice in theoretical literacy, 141–42 n. 37

Reflections on the Revolution in France (Burke), 86, 87, 109
Remiet, Pierre, 57, 58
Representability, 79–80
Representation, 15, 22, 38–39, 42, 132 n. 32; forms of, 4–6, 22–23, 35; limits of, 93, 145–46 n. 77; mimetic, 6–7, 121
Republic (Plato), 3–4, 54, 125–26 n. 4
Reputation, 148 n. 28
Resemblance, 52–53
Revolutionary sublime, 84–88
Rhetoric, 106, 135 n. 18. *See also* Philosophy: rhetoric and
Rhetoric (Aristotle), 50
Ricoeur, Paul, 7, 127 n. 14
Richardson, Samuel, 130 n. 5, 148 n. 33
Rotman, Brian, 56
Rousseau, Jean-Jacques, 111, 140 n. 18
Rule of Metaphor, The (Ricoeur), 127 n. 14

Sanctuary Laws, 150 n. 1
Sandel, Michael, 146 n. 1
Sans papiers, 120–22, 124; the *anomic* and, 120, 150 n. 4; Church of St. Ambroise and, 119, 120; Church of St. Bernard and, 120, 122; mimesis and, 121–22
Schoolman, Mort, 138 n. 59
Sensus communis, 74, 77, 82
Shklar, Judith, 24, 42, 142 n. 40
Sincerity, 101–8
Skinner, Quentin, 25, 26, 31, 131 n. 21
Socrates, 3–4
Sophists, 54
Sovereignty, 37, 122
"Statement of the Voiceless" (World Social Forum), 120

Strong, Tracy B., 130–31 n. 14
Struever, Nancy, 25
Sublime Object of Ideology, The (Žižek), 131–32 n. 29
Supreme Court, exemplarity of, 80–81, 142 n. 44
Surprised by Sin (Fish), 50

Theatrocacy, 9, 128 n. 20
Theoretical literacy: ethics of, 11–12; four-fold grammar of, 10; problem of voice and, 141–42 n. 37
Theory of Justice, A (Rawls), 68–69, 75–76
Thucydides, 26, 32
Tort, aesthetics of, 89–95
Tuck, Richard, 25, 35

Univocity, 56, 58–60, 137 n. 47
Unrepresentability: democratic politics of, 121–23; disequality and, 122; Rancière and, 92

Value, 139 n. 5; credentialing institutions of, 9; culture of, 9; discrimination and, 68–69; public display of, 128 n. 21. *See also* Liberalism: aesthetic value and; Sincerity: value of

Walwyn, William, 22
Weimar Republic, 6, 126 n. 11
What Is the People? (Hazlitt), 112
Winstanley, Gerard, 22
Wolin, Sheldon, 42, 133–34 n. 62
Wordsworth, William, 109
World Social Forum (2003), 120

Zero, concept of, 56–57
Žižek, Slavoj, 131–32 n. 29

DAVIDE PANAGIA

is a Canada Research Chair in Cultural

Studies at Trent University.

Library of Congress Cataloging-in-Publication Data
Panagia, Davide, 1971–
The poetics of political thinking / Davide Panagia.
p. cm.
Includes bibliographical references and index.
ISBN 0-8223-3706-1 (cloth   )
ISBN 0-8223-3718-5 (pbk.   )
1. Political science—Philosophy. 2. Aesthetics,
Modern—Political aspects. I. Title.
JA71.P337 2006
320′.01—dc22   2005027154

www.ingramcontent.com/pod-product-compliance
Lightning Source LLC
Chambersburg PA
CBHW051542230426
43669CB00015B/2691